Dutch Drawings and Watercolors

From the Kharkiv Art Museum

Kristi Nelson

With an Introduction by
Tatyana Prokatova

Taft Museum
Cincinnati

A catalogue of the exhibition at the Taft Museum on view
December 12, 1997, through February 8, 1998

Dutch Drawings and Watercolors from the Kharkiv Art Museum brings to light a collection of works on paper by seventeenth-, eighteenth-, and nineteenth-century masters of land- and seascape, architectural views, still life, and genre. The collection provides a parallel to the Dutch seventeenth- and nineteenth-century oil paintings in the collection of the Taft Museum, while at the same time it offers other media, namely watercolor and drawing. By placing the Taft Museum's collection of Dutch art in a broader context, this exhibition and publication continue the legacy of museum founders Charles and Anna Taft, who held the firm conviction that their collection always be a source of learning and inspiration.

In March 1993 on a visit to Kharkiv, Ukraine, under the auspices of the Cincinnati-Kharkiv Sister City Project, Kristi Nelson, Ph.D., vice provost for faculty relations and professor of art history at the University of Cincinnati, first saw this collection of drawings and watercolors and envisioned the exhibition that accompanies this catalogue. In May 1995 Abby Schwartz, curator of education at the Taft Museum, served as cultural representative to a Cincinnati-Kharkiv Sister City Project delegation to Kharkiv. Her mission during that trip was to put in motion the negotiations for bringing this collection to the Taft Museum. The exhibition and this catalogue are the culmination of that effort.

In bringing this exhibition to Cincinnati, we enhance cultural ties and forge new relationships. Kharkiv Art Museum curators Olga Iosipivna Denisenko and Tatyana Yukhimivna Prokatova, serving as couriers for the exhibition, have been given the opportunity to visit arts institutions in our region, taking back to Kharkiv information about current museum practice in the United States. This exhibition provides the opportunity for collaboration between the University of Cincinnati and the Taft Museum. As curator of the exhibition, Dr. Nelson lends her expertise in Dutch art to the scholarship of this endeavor, uncovering information on a number of artists about whom little has been written to date. This collaboration has also provided the Taft Museum with the opportunity to work closely with the Cincinnati-Kharkiv Sister City Project, an organization that has been heralded internationally as one of the more successful sister city programs.

Our deepest thanks go to Valentina Myzgina, director of the Kharkiv Art Museum, for her generous cooperation and patience in planning this exhibition. Special thanks also to Jack Steinman at Deluxe Engraving for providing the color separations for the catalogue, The David J. Joseph Company for supporting the exhibition, and Hal Wendling at Wendling Printing for the generous donation of printing. We also acknowledge Barbara Gibbs, director of the Cincinnati Art Museum; Kristen Spangenberg, curator of prints and drawings; and Kathryn Haigh, assistant registrar, for graciously lending us the frames for the exhibition. Alexander Etlin was our patient and skillful translator of correspondence and other documents. Fine Arts Fund partner for this exhibition is Cinergy. We thank this company and its employees for their generous annual support of the Taft Museum and the Fine Arts Fund.

Phillip C. Long
Director

Acknowledgments

This project would never have come to fruition without the assistance and kind support of a number of thoughtful individuals. Foremost, I must thank my good friend Professor Egbert Haverkamp-Begemann who brought the Dutch drawings in the Kharkiv Art Museum to my attention. Once he learned that Cincinnati and Kharkiv are sister cities, he encouraged me to study the drawings. Throughout the duration of this project, he has continued to provide wise counsel. My husband, Stewart Goldman, was instrumental in arranging a visit to Kharkiv in March 1993 with the support of the Ohio Arts Council and the Cincinnati-Kharkiv Sister City Project. I am grateful to Dean Jay Chatterjee and the College of Design, Architecture, Art, and Planning (DAAP) at the University of Cincinnati for supporting this trip.

In Kharkiv we were treated royally, and I must thank Valentina Myzgina, director of the Kharkiv Art Museum, who in addition to planning all our activities in Ukraine made viewing the drawings possible, at times under difficult circumstances. Our translator, Michael Petrovitch, was invaluable and navigated us through an unfamiliar language and assisted greatly while viewing the drawings at the museum. Our hosts, Vladimir and Manana Khmel'nitsky, turned over their bedroom to us and sent us off each cold morning warmed by a kasha breakfast.

I am extremely appreciative of the Taft Museum, Director Phillip C. Long, and his staff for seeing the possibility of showing these drawings in Cincinnati and particularly to Assistant Director/Chief Curator David T. Johnson and Curator of Education Abby S. Schwartz for their hard work behind the scenes. Abby, working with the staff of the Kharkiv Art Museum, made the final selection of works for the exhibition and was responsible for all the subsequent dealings with the museum. She carried out an extremely difficult job, especially in dealing with translations and the Ukrainian government, in an outstanding manner. My most sincere thanks are extended to Cate O'Hara, associate curator of public programs and publications, who edited the text with skill and acumen.

Gerbrand Kotting and W. F. Rappard provided assistance at the Rijksbureau voor Kunsthistorische Documentatie (Netherlands Institute for Art History) at The Hague. The staff of the DAAP Library was helpful in procuring materials not available in Cincinnati. Gretchen Shie, one of my graduate students, helped to research the artists' biographies, and to her I am most grateful.

Kristi Nelson
Guest Curator

Tatyana Prokatova
Director, Foreign Art Department, Kharkiv Art Museum

The Kharkiv Art Museum houses the most significant collection in Ukraine of original Dutch drawings of the seventeenth through the nineteenth centuries. The drawings and watercolors by Dutch artists were part of a large art collection formerly belonging to Arkady N. Alfyorov (1812–1872).

This collection was started by Olexander Palitsin (1741–1816), well-known educator, man of letters, and architect. After retirement he settled in the village of Popivka, Sumy District, Kharkiv Province. There, he gathered around himself a circle of progressive-minded gentry and intellectuals of Slobodian (northeastern) Ukraine, which was named the Popivka Academy. Together they conceived the idea of founding a university in Kharkiv, of which Palitsin later served as honorary board member.

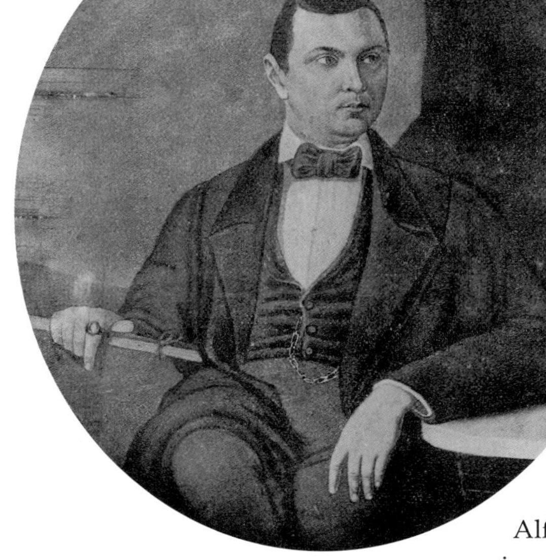

Arkady Nikolayevich Alfyorov, from the portrait painted in oil and formerly on display at the Fine Arts Museum of the Imperial Kharkiv University.

Palitsin amassed a diverse art collection, which was later contributed to by Mykola F. Alfyorov (1760–1848), an architect and active member of the Popivka Academy. Thanks to the financial support of Palitsin and other members, Alfyorov went abroad in 1805 to visit Turkey, Greece, and Italy. There, he purchased a number of paintings and engravings that were added to Palitsin's collection. Alfyorov spent the last years of his life at Popivka, having inherited Palitsin's estate and art collection. After his death the collecting tradition was carried on by his son, Arkady N. Alfyorov.

The younger Alfyorov was born at Popivka. He was raised in the civic-minded cultural atmosphere of the Popivka Academy and received an excellent education at the Imperial Kharkiv University. In addition to artistic talent, he possessed a collector's refined tastes. Collecting, however, was not his primary objective. His aim was to contribute to community art education. "Everyone should work to the best of their abilities to benefit the motherland and home community," Alfyorov wrote in 1858. A man of diverse interests, refined connoisseur, and passionate collector of art, Alfyorov spent all his income creating a library and acquiring paintings, drawings, and engravings.

Because of his health, from 1857 until the end of his life, Alfyorov lived in Germany, where he successfully expanded his collection. He visited Berlin, Leipzig, Dresden, Aachen, and Bonn. His illness was progressing, however, and he died in 1872. His executor (a hospital director in Bonn where Alfyorov died) implemented his will exactly: in 1873 the entire collection was donated to the Fine Arts Museum of the Imperial Kharkiv University, one of the direct predecessors of the Kharkiv Art Museum.

Overview

The art historian Hendrick Enno van Gelder noted that one of the important contributions of the Netherlands has been its rich bounty of talented artists, including painters and draftsmen, who have added significantly to the country's cultural heritage.[1] The exhibition of Dutch drawings from the Kharkiv Art Museum, Ukraine, is indicative of this phenomenon and affords the opportunity to view together works on paper produced during three centuries of Dutch art as well as to confront the tastes of the Ukrainian collector Arkady N. Alfyorov (1812–1872). Despite the fact that Kharkiv possesses no works by Rembrandt van Rijn (1606–1669) or Vincent van Gogh (1853–1890), the exhibition brings to the forefront drawings and watercolors that have remained relatively unknown until now by a variety of outstanding Dutch artists.

Historically, the Dutch Republic emerged in 1579 when seven of the northern provinces of the Netherlandish territories declared their independence from Philip II (1527–1598), the Hapsburg king of Spain, who ruled them through a governor in Brussels. The movement was led primarily by Protestant leaders—local nobles, ecclesiastics, and rich merchants— in the north who wanted to break away from Catholic Spain. Philip II and the Spanish governors of the southern Netherlands resisted this movement and did not officially recognize the United Provinces until 1648 when the Eighty Years' War ended with the Peace of Münster, although some peace had been enjoyed since 1609 when the Twelve Years' Truce was concluded with the Spanish at Antwerp.

During the seventeenth century—the Golden Age of Dutch art—innumerable artists produced works of high artistic quality and beauty. This was a time when a common political purpose created economic advantage to make the Dutch Republic one of the more influential commercial and maritime powers in all Europe. With increasing prosperity the market for pictures and other works of art, including drawings, grew tremendously despite the lack of patronage from Catholic and Protestant churches or a strong monarchy. Eager to display newfound wealth, middle-class citizens ordered drawings and paintings directly from artists or bought them from dealers, book and picture shops, or fairs. Increasing demand on the open market caused specialization of subject matter for which the seventeenth century is famous, including history, portraiture, landscape, genre, marine, architectural interiors, and still life.

The Dutch Republic remained strong and prosperous throughout the eighteenth century despite the expanding power of Great Britain and France, while the art produced at this time was a reflection of earlier achievements. In 1795 the armies of revolutionary France imposed a pro-French government, and in 1810 France annexed the Netherlands. With the defeat of Napoléon Bonaparte in 1814–15, the present Dutch state, called the Kingdom of the Netherlands, came into being. Originally Belgium was part of this union, but it seceded in 1830 and became an independent nation. The art market remained healthy throughout the eighteenth century, which also witnessed the rise of the professional collector of drawings. The nineteenth century is marked by a liberalization of the government, the establishment of several art schools, and the introduction of a number of artistic movements and social reforms. At this time art societies, such as the Dutch Drawing Society, were important in assisting artists to market their work.

The Kharkiv drawings, like paintings, were nearly all produced as finished works intended for sale and are a testament to the role that drawing played in the stylistic development of Dutch art from the seventeenth through the nineteenth centuries. Dutch texts from this time, however, are brief on artists' statements about the intent and nature of drawing, and other printed sources likewise have little to say on the matter. It was not until about 1850 that Dutch artists began to publish their feelings toward art and what inspired them to be artists. Even then comments on drawing are limited and tend to be connected more with art in general, which was also the case in seventeenth-century writings. Both artist and writer, Karel van Mander stressed the importance of drawing well in his *Foundations of the Noble Free Art of Painting (Grondt der edel vry schilderkonst)* published in 1604.[2] Willem Goeree, in his short book *Introduction to the General Art of Drawing (Inleyding tot de al-ghemeene teycken-konst),* the one exception to this lack of specific texts on drawing, refers to drawing as the basis of all other arts and also compares drawing and painting to poetry.[3] The former concept continued through the nineteenth century when one theme that remained central in writings was that drawing is the "Mother of all Arts."[4]

Drawing has long been regarded as one of the direct means through which an artist responds to and records the visible world. The drawings from Kharkiv reveal the veneration that nineteenth-century Dutch artists had for those who had preceded them and whose work frequently served as meaningful points of reference for their own art. Many of the traditions and areas of subject matter established during the seventeenth century remained imbedded in the Dutch artistic spirit and continued to inspire artists for the next two centuries. Certainly a theme that links all the works is the portrayal by Dutch artists of their land and people. This they did with lifelike qualities that have attracted artists, collectors, and spectators throughout the centuries.

This realism, as it is now called, reflects a study of nature that prevailed for at least three centuries in various forms and is characterized by precise documentation and keen observation. The Kharkiv works on paper testify that this approach is always integrally connected with high quality drawing distinguished by the use of eloquent lines, powerful brushstrokes, and atmospheric tonal values, while color becomes an integral component that adds to the naturalism of those pieces created in watercolor. They demonstrate the capacity for passionate observation on the part of Dutch artists in the representation of landscape, townscape, cattle pieces, genre, and still-life subject matter and the consistency with which they took pride in the representation of everyday objects and events. Seventeenth-century texts—especially those by Van Mander, Philips Angel, and Samuel van Hoogstraten—provide a good description for a great deal of Dutch painting of this period and reference the representation of pleasant images that are deceptively real, capture beauty, entice the eye, and thereby conquer nature.[5] One could reasonably argue, as is clearly evident in the works themselves, that these concepts are analogous with the qualities present in the Kharkiv drawings.

Beyond thematic and visual links, the connections that exist among the artists represented in the collection are tremendously rich. For example, the style of Pieter Molijn (cat. 22) is close to that of Jan van Goyen (compare cat. 11), and the former may have been the teacher of Allaert van Everdingen (cats. 8, 9). Among the nineteenth-century artists

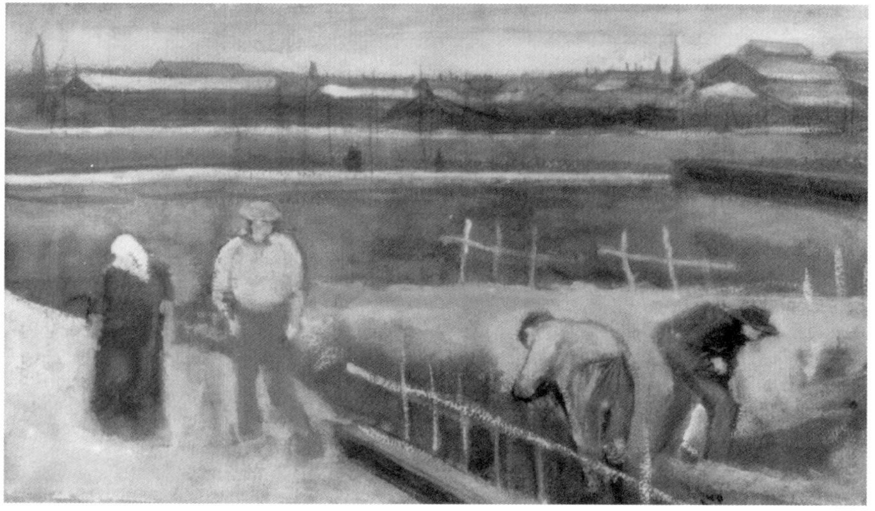

Figure 1. Vincent van Gogh's watercolor *Working in the Fields* captures the interest of nineteenth-century artists in the quick sketch and observing from nature in a fresh way.

represented, David Joseph Bles (cat. 3),
Johannes Bosboom (cat. 4), and Desirée Oscar
Léopold von Franckenberg en Proschlitz (cat.
10) were all members of the Pulchri Studio in
The Hague. Andreas Schelfhout (cat. 28) gave
art lessons to Anton Braakman (cat. 5), Jan
Frans Hoppenbrouwers (cat. 12), and Jacobus
Adrianus Vrolijk (cat. 34). Bles was a close
friend of Jan Weissenbruch (cat. 36).
Bosboom, Samuel Verveer (cat. 33), and
Petrus Gerardus Vertin (cat. 31) all studied in
The Hague with Bartholomeus Johannes van
Hove (1790–1880). Whether Alfyorov
considered these connections as he built his
collection or whether he acquired them for
other reasons is not known; nevertheless,
it makes for fascinating study and analysis
today.

Importance of Drawings

It was during the seventeenth century in
the Netherlands that drawings began to be collected and commissioned for themselves, as
opposed to their more traditional function as preparatory studies for finished works in
various media.[6] At this time all kinds of subjects began to appear in drawings, paralleling
the development in painting, and drawings stand as complete works that were made and
sold as finished objects. The landscape drawings of Van Everdingen, the follower of Van
Goyen, and Molijn were nearly all signed, often dated, and made as independent works
intended for sale.

In the literature on seventeenth-century art, two important concepts are usually
discussed that can be related to the creative force in drawings: *naer het leven* (from life) and
uyt den geest (from memory).[7] During the sixteenth century these two approaches were
connected to subject matter—religious and mythological scenes were drawn from the
imagination, while figure studies could have been based on the live model and took the
form of an exercise. During the seventeenth century the *naer het leven* concept acquired
greater significance, particularly because the final appearance of the work was important.
In this case preparatory drawings from life could be used directly, but drawings from
memory were frequently shaped by drawing from life.

Nowhere is this more evident than in the seventeenth-century landscape drawings (cats.
8, 9, 11, 18, 22, and 35), in which their natural look suggests they were drawn from nature
when they may have been drawn from memory. Most Dutch landscape artists traveled, if
not abroad at least in their own environs, and drew in the countryside or kept sketchbooks,
all of which trained them to be able to draw naturalistically from memory. It is well
documented that Rembrandt took walks around Amsterdam and made sketches of the city
and its environs. Back in the studio where the finished drawings were produced, the artist
could rearrange nature to create verisimilitude with the chosen subject matter. Landscape
artists presented not reality itself but a plausible view of Dutch surroundings based on
drawing from nature and from memory. Thus, it is sometimes difficult to differentiate

Figure 2. Jacob van Ruisdael's *Farmhouses on a High Road* is a carefully constructed invention produced in the studio. Ruisdael's landscapes influenced later artists with their artful compositions that create harmony among trees, land, sky, atmosphere, and light.

which drawings were done from life and which from memory—but it is the combination that distinguishes the drawings of this century.

Similarly, the one figure drawing by Herman Saftleven II (cat. 27) and the anonymous still life of traveling equipment (cat. 1) probably began as studies from the imagination but appear highly naturalistic, since drawing from life laid the foundation for drawing from memory. Both point to the significant role that drawing played in the creation of the naturalistic look of Dutch art in general during the seventeenth century.[8]

During the eighteenth century appreciation of drawing as an independent branch of art continued to grow. The interest on the part of collectors in drawn copies of seventeenth-century paintings necessitated that color be added to drawings, and the preference for highly detailed works gave prestige to the colored drawing.[9] Making copies and adding color to reproductions thereby created additional income for many artists. The artist and draftsman Isaac de Moucheron (cat. 23, pl.VIII) made a specialty of this type of work, sometimes adding color and his signature to original seventeenth-century landscape drawings but more frequently producing his own watercolor creations to meet the demand for colored and finished works.[10] Dirk Maes (cat. 20, pl. VII), whose work spans both the seventeenth and eighteenth centuries, produced highly finished colored drawings that featured horses and Italianate landscape settings. Although only a few eighteenth-century pieces are represented in the exhibition, throughout the century the importance of drawing well continued to be upheld, since drawing was considered to be essential for all other forms of art. As a result numerous tuition-free drawing schools were established to train students for all types of industrial and artistic work.[11]

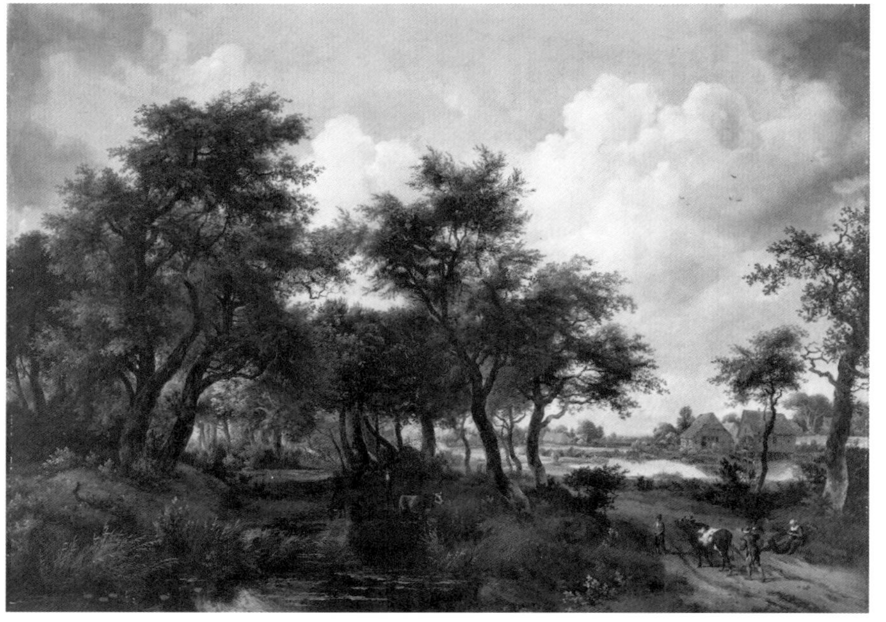

Figure 3. *Farmland with a Pond and Trees* by Meyndert Hobbema reveals a naturalistic breadth and continuity of view that reflects his admiration for the work of Jacob van Ruisdael. The light reflected on the water in the foreground, the tree trunks silhouetted against the open horizon in the middle ground, and the sunlight on the open spaces to the right easily move the viewer's eye through the carefully arranged space.

It can be ascertained that at the beginning of the nineteenth century the carefully detailed, colored, and finished drawing remained the choice of collectors, despite the lack of written statements about the ideas of eighteenth- and nineteenth-century artists and collectors regarding types of drawing and drawing styles. Watercolors, pastels, and large detailed drawings that had been collectors' items since the seventeenth century remained popular. However, as the comments of the artist and collector Cornelis Ploos van Amstel (1726–1798) disclose, there was growing interest in the quick sketch because of its immediacy and revelation of the more direct thoughts of the artist.[12] From the middle of the nineteenth century, this trend was to continue, and people began to appreciate more consistently the sketch and rough drawing. Barend Cornelis Koekkoek (1803–1862) commented on the need for an artist to constantly sketch and make studies from nature in his *Revelations of a Landscape Artist,*[13] while Van Gogh stressed the importance of continually observing from nature in a fresh way (fig. 1).[14] Willem Roelofs (cat. 26) urged artists to use nature as a guide and capture the impression of the moment.[15]

Watercolors remained in wide public demand throughout the second half of the nineteenth century, as is evident in Alfyorov's own collecting habits and in pieces selected for the exhibition: more than half of the thirty-six works were executed in watercolor. It was Anton Mauve (cat. 21) who recommended to Van Gogh that he should perfect the watercolor technique in order to make a living. Meanwhile in Amsterdam the artists' society Arti et Amicitiae promoted an appreciation for watercolor and works on paper through art viewings.[16] Bosboom and Roelofs were among the first members to join The Hague's Pulchri Studio, which was founded in 1847 to enable its members to practice life drawing, to discuss each other's work, and to provide a place for artists to socialize. From it the Dutch Drawing Society (De Hollandsche Teken Maatschappij) was established in 1876, which also abetted the market for watercolors. It was modeled on the Belgian Watercolor Society established in 1856 and the older, more elite English Watercolour Society, which had been in existence since 1804. Within two years a number of artists—Bles, Bosboom, Jozef Israëls (cat. 13, pl. V), Mauve, Elchanon Verveer (cat. 32), and Weissenbruch—had been included as members, and the society was considered an unqualified success. It remained so until the 1890s when the artists came under strong criticism and the demand for works in watercolor paled in comparison with interest in pieces that emphasized precision of line.[17]

Thanks to the presence of Willem Roelofs in Brussels, Dutch watercolors with their skillfulness and accuracy of technique were also highly regarded by the Belgian public and collectors. Bosboom, Israëls, Mauve, and Bles enjoyed great popularity there.

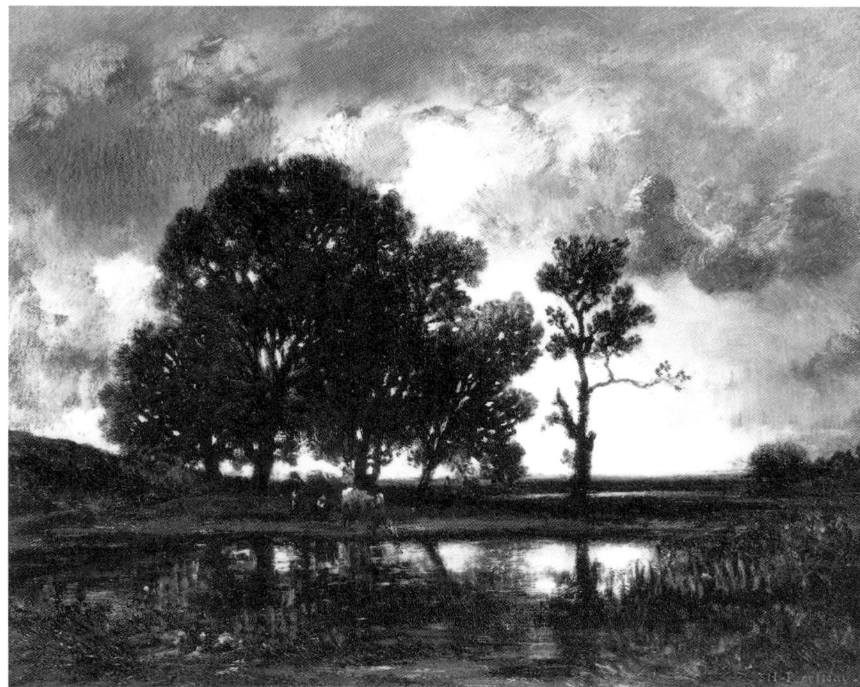

Figure 4. Influential for the Hague School artists, Pierre-Etienne-Théodore Rousseau was adept at manipulating the mood in his paintings by varying the time of day and weather conditions. In *The Pond* the small pool catches the last rays of the setting sun, which silhouettes the massive oaks dwarfing the figures beneath the dramatic sky.

Landscape

The predominance of landscape in the exhibition attests not only to Alfyorov's tastes but also to the place of land and country in the Dutch consciousness. Obviously, many artists were taken with the act of portraying the beauty of nature, and it is not surprising that some of the more original contributions of Dutch art were made in the area of landscape.

A large number of landscape drawings were produced during the seventeenth century. The Kharkiv examples provide a clear picture of the growth of the realistic Dutch landscape through the statements of Molijn, the follower of Van Goyen, and Van Everdingen. Earlier in the century landscapes had generally been tied to topographical representation, as in the work of Hendrik Goltzius (1558–1617) or Claes Jansz. Visscher (1587–1652), or were connected to the world landscape of the sixteenth century. These later artists, however, introduced a landscape that portrays the Dutch countryside or more accurately recreates a Dutch landscape with its dunes, water, vistas, and distinctively cloudy sky. In the studio they selected and rearranged nature to achieve the right balance, harmony, and tonality for the composition and to depict something that was attractive and pleasing to the eye while maintaining truth to the native Dutch countryside. Later in the century, the more fully developed forest scene by Antonis Waterloo (cat. 35) demonstrates the weight and power of nature as developed most eloquently by Jacob van Ruisdael

(1628/29–1682) as well as its beauty (fig. 2).

Eighteenth-century landscapes tended to emulate the style developed during the seventeenth century with sources found in the Dutch countryside and the seasons. Stylistically, the work of Ruisdael and Meyndert Hobbema (1638–1709) served as important points of reference with an emphasis on an active play of trees and branches (fig. 3). During the eighteenth century the topographical drawing rose to prominence again, and many of the works produced provide valuable source material on Dutch towns. Toward the end of the century, a group of artists including Gillis Smak Gregoor (cat. 29) looked for inspiration to the landscape pictures with cows by Albert Cuyp (1620–1691) either directly or through the intermediary Abraham van Strij (1753–1826).[18]

A group of landscape artists was active in Amsterdam during 1810–30, among them Hendrik Gerrit ten Cate (cat. 6, pl. III). As in his watercolor in the exhibition, landscapes in these years tended to have a slightly more classical look with compositions controlled through careful placement of horizontal and vertical lines. A lighter touch is evident in the application of soft gray and brown washes and pale watercolor tones.

Thereafter, from 1830 until the end of the century, The Hague became the landscape center for both painting and drawing. As early as 1820 Andreas Schelfhout was highly regarded as a draftsman; both his prolific output and subject matter were influential throughout the nineteenth century. Although Schelfhout and his pupils, such as Adrianus Vrolijk, came under the influence of French Romantic work, especially through prints and lithographs, they added elements more true to the Dutch tradition including a stronger realistic tendency and less emphasis on the narrative aspects of romanticism.[19] While the style that emerged in their work is frequently qualified as Dutch Romantic, the key components included an emphasis on looseness of drawing (a more painterly quality perhaps), curving lines, and a sense for harmonic composition. Many of these artists also looked back to the seventeenth century and were attracted to the landscapes of Ruisdael and Waterloo. Subject matter tended to include scenes based on the seasons—as in Hoppenbrouwers's *Autumn Landscape* (cat. 12) or Braakman's *Winter Scene* (cat. 5)—cityscapes, and water scenes such as Schelfhout's *Windmill and Boat in a Landscape* (cat. 28). On the whole drawings produced during the Dutch Romantic era have a quieter, more serene mood than French Romantic pieces with their more volcanic emotional content.

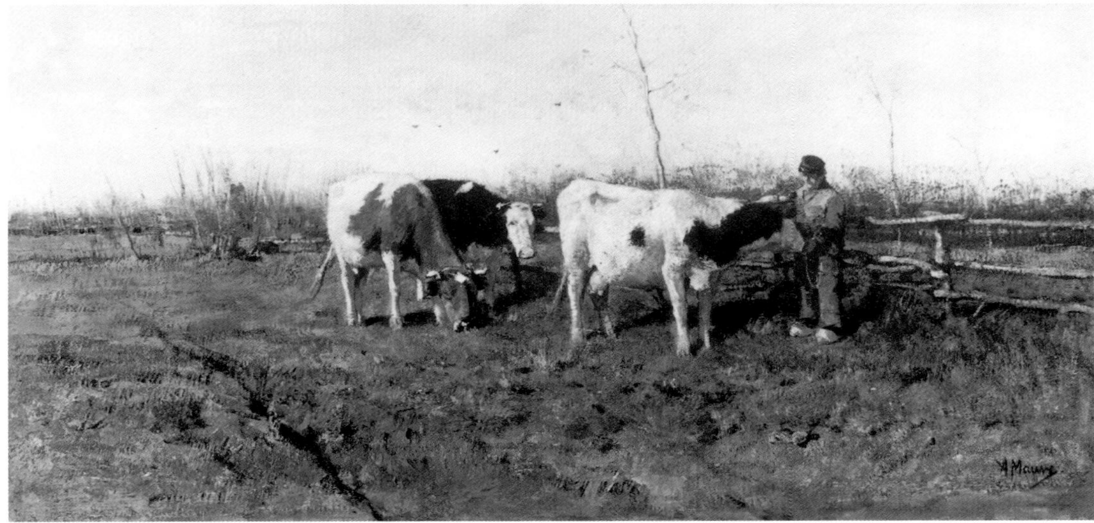

Figure 5. Anton Mauve's preferred motif was domesticated animals situated in landscape settings marked by vast countryside, low horizon, and monochromatic sky. In *Cattle Grazing* the careful positioning of the cows and man below the horizon emphasizes their connection to the natural world.

The so-called Romantic style remained in fashion until about 1860 when the French Barbizon School became known in the Netherlands. Under this influence artists attempted to capture a momentary impression of the landscape that had a poetic yet pictorial character. In 1851 Willem Roelofs was the first of the painters from The Hague to visit Barbizon, where he was attracted to the treatment of light and natural handling of figures by Pierre-Etienne-Théodore Rousseau (1812–1867; fig. 4). Jan Weissenbruch was also among its early proponents, with Johannes Bosboom, Anton Mauve, and Jacob Maris (1837–1899) eventually forming the core of the Hague School artists who painted a great number of landscapes.[20] In general these artists used light and shade, tonal values, and limited color to capture the various moods of the Dutch landscape and weather with its cloudy skies, hazy horizon, flat meadows, dunes, and gray seas.

Cattle Pieces

Closely related to the landscape artists are the specialists in cattle pieces. This genre rose to prominence during the seventeenth century with artists such as Paulus Potter (1625–1654), Adriaen van de Velde (1636–1672), and Albert Cuyp but was hardly present in the art of the eighteenth century. During the nineteenth century the subject resurfaced, and the veneration for the previous century can be detected in the work of Simon van den Berg (cat. 2), Smak Gregoor, Ten Cate, and Jan van Ravenswaay (cat. 25). Van Ravenswaay was a native of Hilversum where a number of painters of cattle and sheep came to work, creating a kind of artists' colony there and in nearby 's-Graveland.[21] Subject matter was readily available because many sheep and cows were raised in the area's woods and meadows. Van den Berg worked primarily in The Hague, which also boasted a number of artists of cattle and sheep. Mauve, whose watercolor *Cows* (cat. 21) is included in the exhibition, liked to work in the area of Oosterbeek, a village in eastern Gelderland, which attracted many artists and writers because of its picturesque surroundings of heathland and parklike woods (fig. 5).[22]

Townscapes, Interiors, Seascapes, and Still Life

During the seventeenth century Holland's commercial prosperity was evident in its towns, which were an expression of a fierce pride in the country's achievement—as Sir William Temple observed while the English ambassador to The Hague during the late 1660s and the 1670s.[23] Although towns or parts of them had a long history of representation in art, it was in the seventeenth century that a realistic account of the way buildings are seen in towns developed. Those city- or townscapes that were produced during the seventeenth century by artists such as Jan van der Heyden (1637–1712) have as their principle focus the view of a certain city or its streets. This differs from the *veduta*, a more exact reproduction of a topographical situation, which was popular during the eighteenth century in Venice and elsewhere in Europe. The interest in topographical views tended to die out during the nineteenth century, and instead artists preferred to depict cityscapes, often in the historical center of a town, with an interest in creating atmosphere rather than a specific view of a street or building. On the whole the work of artists who painted

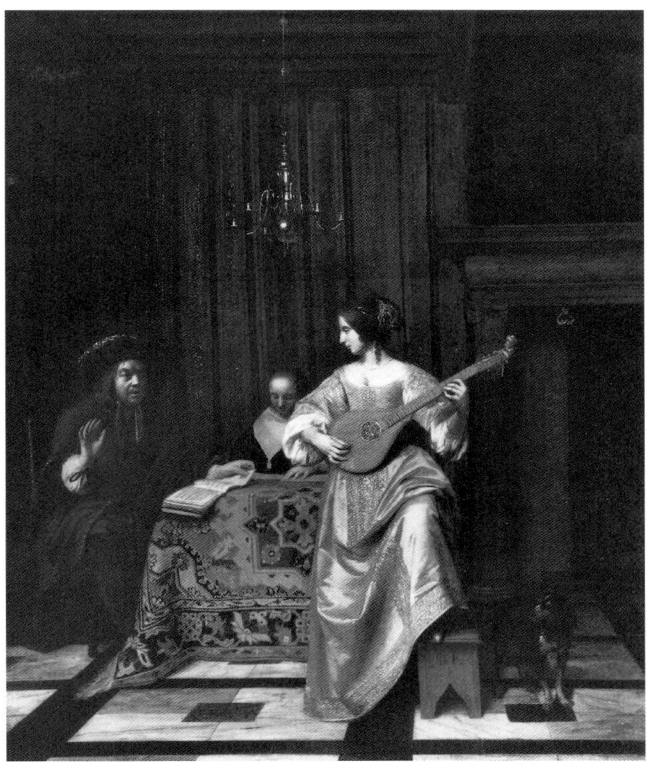

Figure 6. Typical of seventeenth-century Dutch genre pictures, Pieter de Hooch's *A Woman with a Cittern and a Singing Couple at a Table* is not based on literature but creates an image of everyday middle-class life set within a realistically detailed interior. Many later artists looked to this kind of non-narrative picture as they revived genre painting in the nineteenth century.

cityscapes falls into the Dutch Romantic phase given their style of drawing. Samuel Verveer's *Town View* (cat. 33), Vertin's *Market in Winter* (cat. 31), and Weissenbruch's *On the Square* (cat. 36) represent the development of this genre in the medium of watercolor in The Hague. On the other hand the church interior depicted by Bosboom (cat. 4) can now be identified with specificity as the Saint Laurenskerk at Rotterdam.

Marine views, seascapes, and ships were represented in Dutch art for more than three and a half centuries from about 1550 to 1900 and reflect the essential role that water and shipping have played in the history of Holland. Two seascapes from Kharkiv are included in the exhibition. The drawing by Willem van de Velde the Younger (cat. 30) is an excellent example of the drawing style practiced by the Van de Velde family of artists in the latter part of the seventeenth century. Both the elder and younger Van de Veldes were prolific draftsmen and used drawings to provide information that could be adapted during different stages of painting to form the final image. The *Seascape* by Hermanus Koekkoek (cat. 16) shows a calm sea. Only a few artists depicted seascapes in the nineteenth century, and Koekkoek can be identified with the Romantic influence that characterized landscapes during the first half of the century.

Still life was yet another specialty category that developed its own independent identity during the seventeenth century. Netherlandish artists, however, had long been highly respected for their depiction of fruits, flowers, and other still-life elements. At the end of the eighteenth century, a number of draftsmen specialized in fruit and flower

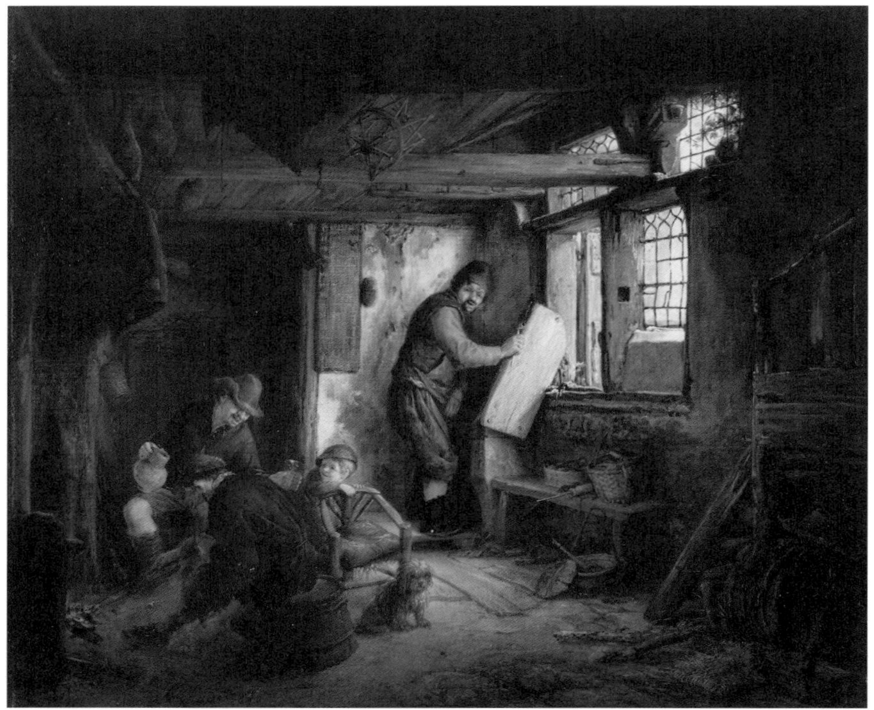

Figure 7. Scenes depicting aspects of Dutch peasant life, such as Adriaen van Ostade's *Interior of an Inn with Three Men and a Boy*, influenced later artists who staged their scenes in seventeenth-century interiors complete with historic costume and accouterment.

still lifes, working primarily in watercolor. Most were inspired by the famous eighteenth-century flower painter Jan van Huysum (1682–1749), including Georgius Jacobus Johannes van Os, whose *Flower Bouquet* (cat. 24, cover) is included in the exhibition. Although presented naturalistically and seemingly real, there is always an artifice to flower still lifes. In general not all the flowers in a painted or drawn arrangement would naturally be in bloom at one time. Further, artists tended to depict more flowers than a vase could actually hold and thus presented an arrangement that is more conceptual than real.

Genre

The illustration of literary themes was never popular in the Netherlands during the nineteenth century, and when around 1830 genre scenes of everyday life increased in popularity, artists looked to seventeenth-century painters such as Nicolaes Maes (1634–1693) and Pieter de Hooch (1629–1684) for ideas and subject matter (fig. 6). The rise of genre in seventeenth-century Holland has been well documented and the nature of its realism explored by various scholars.[24] Especially of interest in the literature has been the dual role of pleasure and instruction afforded by the realistic representation of the non-

narrative scenes of everyday life. In seventeenth-century genre
paintings and drawings, it can be argued that a moral is present
but not always as a didactic warning. By the nineteenth century
any moral tone has generally disappeared from the genre pieces
although the historical precedents cannot be dismissed.

Genre representations of the nineteenth century vary: in
some pieces costumes and attributes are difficult to date, while
in other instances artists faithfully adhered to seventeenth- or
eighteenth-century settings. In this vein the work of David
Joseph Bles is often referred to as "historical genre" in its
evocation of a seventeenth-century setting. The subject of his
Woman with a Spinning Wheel (cat. 3, pl. I) should be compared
to the drawing by Jan Luyken (cat. 19) because both deal with
the theme of spinning. Likewise, Herman Frederik Carel ten
Kate was greatly influenced by Adriaen van Ostade (1610–1685;
fig. 7) and Adriaen Brouwer (1606–1638), and his *Soldier's Story*
(cat. 14, pl. VI) is staged in a seventeenth-century interior. The
watercolors by Willem Cornelis van Dijk (cat. 7, pl. IV) and
Desirée Oscar Léopold von Franckenberg en Proschlitz (cat. 10)
depict themes frequently found in seventeenth-century genre
paintings, drawings, and prints.

The watercolor by Jozef Israëls illustrating the death of a
fisherman reflects his interest in capturing the life of fisherfolk
(cat. 13, pl. V). It should be remembered that Israëls traveled to
Barbizon not for its scenery but to study rural life and its human
element (fig. 8). In *Fisherman's Death* he shows himself to be a master of watercolor in his
use of soft washes, muted color, and dark tone to create the appropriate mood for the
subject. The work clearly demonstrates the extent to which Dutch artists had mastered the
technique of watercolor and realized its fullest potential as a medium.

It is through the work of Israëls that we come to grips with the powerful connections
that give Dutch drawing its identity and unique character. The drawings from Kharkiv
demonstrate how clearly Netherlandish artists were dependent on nature for source
material but through the imagination turned images of everyday life into pieces of great
beauty. Therein lies the attraction of the drawings and watercolors in the exhibition and
a factor in Dutch art that must have appealed to Arkady N. Alfyorov as he was building
his collection.

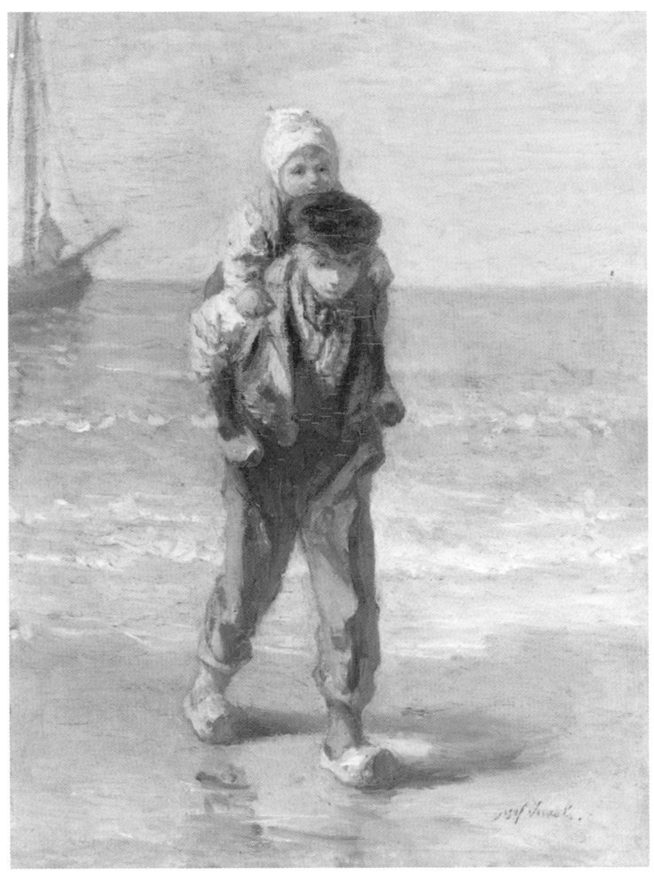

Figure 8. *Pick-a-Back* by
Jozef Israëls reflects his
interest in rural life and the
human element. The
atmosphere, loose
brushwork, and handling of
light contribute to the sense
of timelessness of the boy
in fisherman's garb carrying
his sibling along the shore.

NOTES

1. Van Gelder.

2. Schatborn, pp. 11–12.

3. Ibid., p. 12.

4. Te Rijdt, in Rotterdam 1994, p. 24.

5. Sluijter, pp. 175–207.

6. Schatborn, in Robinson and Schatborn, p. 7.

7. Ibid., pp. 7– 12.

8. Westerman, pp. 7–15.

9. Niemeijer, p. 8.

10. Broos, pp. 34–55.

11. Te Rijdt, in Rotterdam 1994, p. 24.

12. Ibid., pp. 24–25.

13. De Bodt, in Rotterdam 1995, p. 24.

14. Vincent van Gogh to Theo van Gogh, The Hague, Dec. 1882; see Van Gogh I, p. 495.

15. De Bodt, in Rotterdam 1995, p. 25.

16. De Leeuw, pp. 24–25.

17. De Bodt, in Rotterdam 1995, pp. 26–30.

18. Te Rijdt, in Rotterdam 1994, pp. 27–28.

19. On Dutch Romanticism see Sillevis, pp. 4–6, and Knoef.

20. For the Hague School see De Gruyter and De Leeuw.

21. Te Rijdt, in Rotterdam 1994, p. 29.

22. De Leeuw, pp. 56–60.

23. Wattenmaker, p. 15.

24. On genre painting see Sutton 1984. For didactic and disguised meanings, see Sluijter, and for aspects of domesticity with regard to the genre drawings in the exhibition, see Franits.

FIGURES

1. Vincent van Gogh (1853–1890), *Travaux des champs (Working in the Fields)*, 1882, watercolor, 311 x 514 mm (12½ x 20¼ in.). Private collection.

2. Jacob van Ruisdael (1628/29–1682), *Farmhouses on a High Road*, about 1658–60, oil on canvas, 57.5 x 67.9 cm (22⅝ x 26¾ in.). Taft Museum, bequest of Mr. and Mrs. Charles Phelps Taft, 1931.391.

3. Meyndert Hobbema (1638–1709), *Farmland with a Pond and Trees*, about 1663–64, oil on canvas, 96.5 x 128.3 cm (38 x 50½ in.). Taft Museum, bequest of Mr. and Mrs. Charles Phelps Taft, 1931.407.

4. Pierre-Etienne-Théodore Rousseau (1812–1867), *The Pond*, 1844?, oil on canvas, 38.7 x 46.7 cm (15¼ x 18⅜ in.). Taft Museum, bequest of Mr. and Mrs. Charles Phelps Taft, 1931.429.

5. Anton Mauve (1838–1888), *Cattle Grazing*, late 1870s, oil on canvas, 34.3 x 70.5 cm (13½ x 27¾ in.). Taft Museum, bequest of Mr. and Mrs. Charles Phelps Taft, 1931.411.

6. Pieter de Hooch (1629–1684), *A Woman with a Cittern and a Singing Couple at a Table*, about 1667, oil on canvas, 70.8 x 57.9 cm (27⅞ x 22¾ in.). Taft Museum, bequest of Mr. and Mrs. Charles Phelps Taft, 1931.395.

7. Adriaen van Ostade (1610–1685), *Interior of an Inn with Three Men and a Boy*, 1656, oil on panel, 33.8 x 39.5 cm (13¼ x 15½ in.). Taft Museum, bequest of Mr. and Mrs. Charles Phelps Taft, 1931.400.

8. Jozef Israëls (1824–1911), *Pick-a-Back*, about 1872, oil on panel, 30.2 x 21.7 cm (11⅞ x 8½ in.). Taft Museum, bequest of Mr. and Mrs. Charles Phelps Taft, 1931.428.

Holland, seventeenth century

1. *Things for Traveling*

Pen and gray wash with traces of black chalk, 152 x 247 mm (6 x 9¾ in.)*

The traditional attribution to Willem Kalf (1619–1693) is in all likelihood not correct.[1] The objects in the drawing—a small valise, knapsack, bucket, hat, cup, and saucer—are all items associated with the theme of travel. It is thematically related to a painting by Paulus Bor (1600–1659), now in a private collection in Canada, which portrays a still life with chest, saddlebag, open book, and other objects on a table before a window in a monastic setting.[2] Further connection can be drawn to a rare etching dated about 1650 by Leonard Bramer (1596–1674) showing a traveling box, an example of which is in the Art Institute of Chicago.[3] All three—drawing, painting, and print—derive from the same topos and belong to a small group of seventeenth-century Dutch still-life pieces that depict travel equipment as a genre. The prominent placement of the musket in this drawing suggests that travel during the seventeenth century could be fraught with danger.

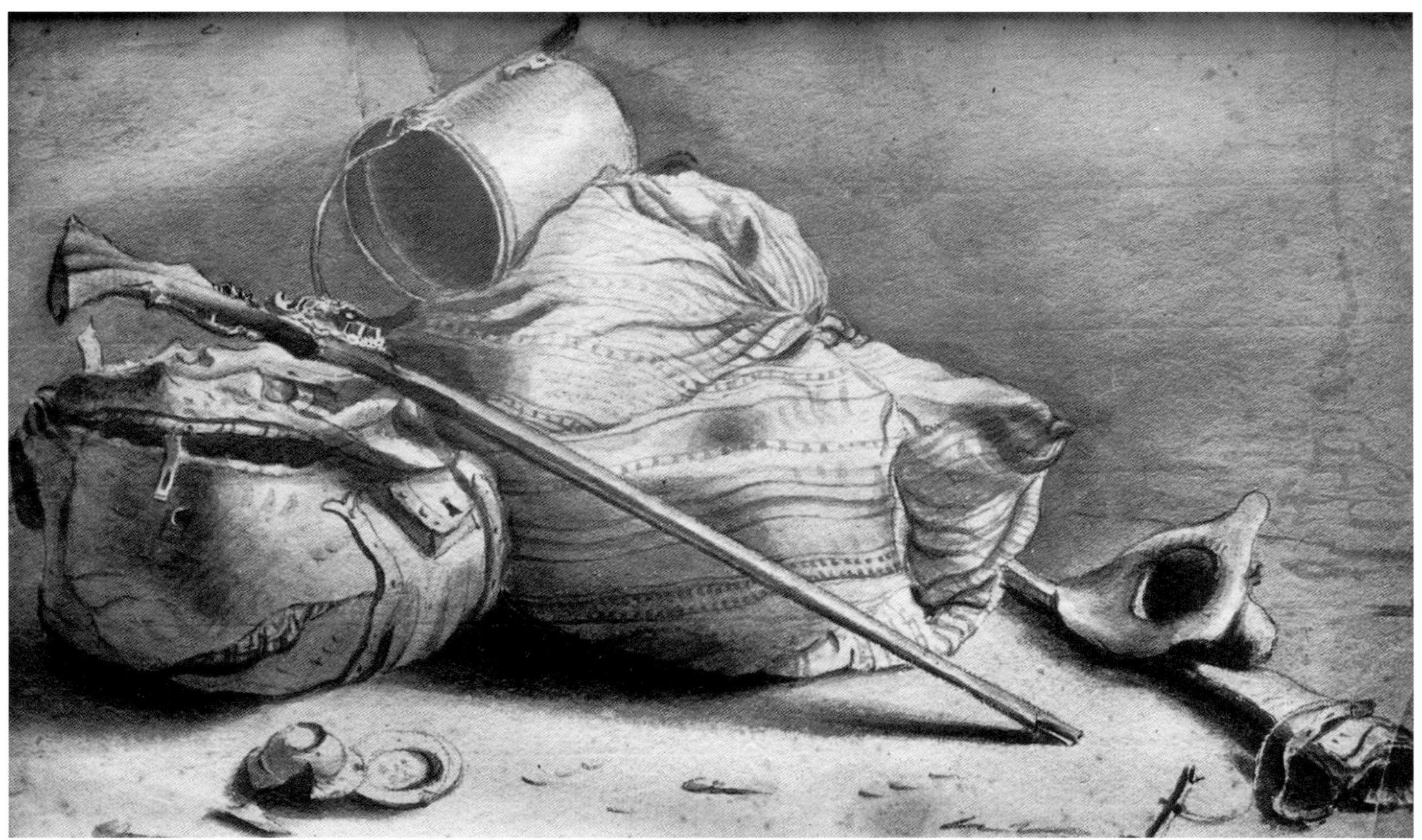

Notes

*Height proceeds width in all dimensions.

1. I am indebted to Professor Egbert Haverkamp-Begemann for his assistance with this drawing and the references to Bor and Bramer.

2. Oil on panel, 56 x 76 cm (22 x 30 in.), signed and dated on an open book: *P. Bor 1630*. See Feigen, no. 6.

3. *Still Life with Traveling Theme*, 13.6 x 18.6 cm (5⅜ x 7½ in.), acc. no. 1940.92. See Hollstein III, p. 183 (Wurzbach: L. Bramer, no. 4).

Overschie (near Rotterdam) 1812–1891 The Hague

2. *Sheep in a Landscape*

Brown wash, 179 x 253 mm (7⅛ x 10 in.)
Signed lower left: S *van den Berg f*

Simon van den Berg painted animals and landscapes. He studied at the Rotterdam Academy under Jacob de Meijer (1798–1884) and at The Hague with Pieter Gerardus van Os (1776–1839) along with Wouterus Verschuur (1812–1874) and Jan van Ravenswaay (cat. 25). He became an influential teacher at the The Hague Academy. In 1875 he became the keeper of collections at the Mauritshuis in The Hague and from 1880 to 1889 served as its director. Major collections of his drawings are found in the Rijksprentenkabinet at Amsterdam, the Teylers Stichting at Haarlem, the Museum Boymans-van Beuningen at Rotterdam, and the Gemeentemuseum at The Hague.

Most of Van den Berg's work depicts cows and sheep at pasture and as in this drawing reflects the influence of Paulus Potter (1625–1654), transmitted though Van den Berg's teacher Van Os. In this drawing the handling of the sheep on the left and the use of light and shade to suggest their thick unshorn coats are particularly effective.

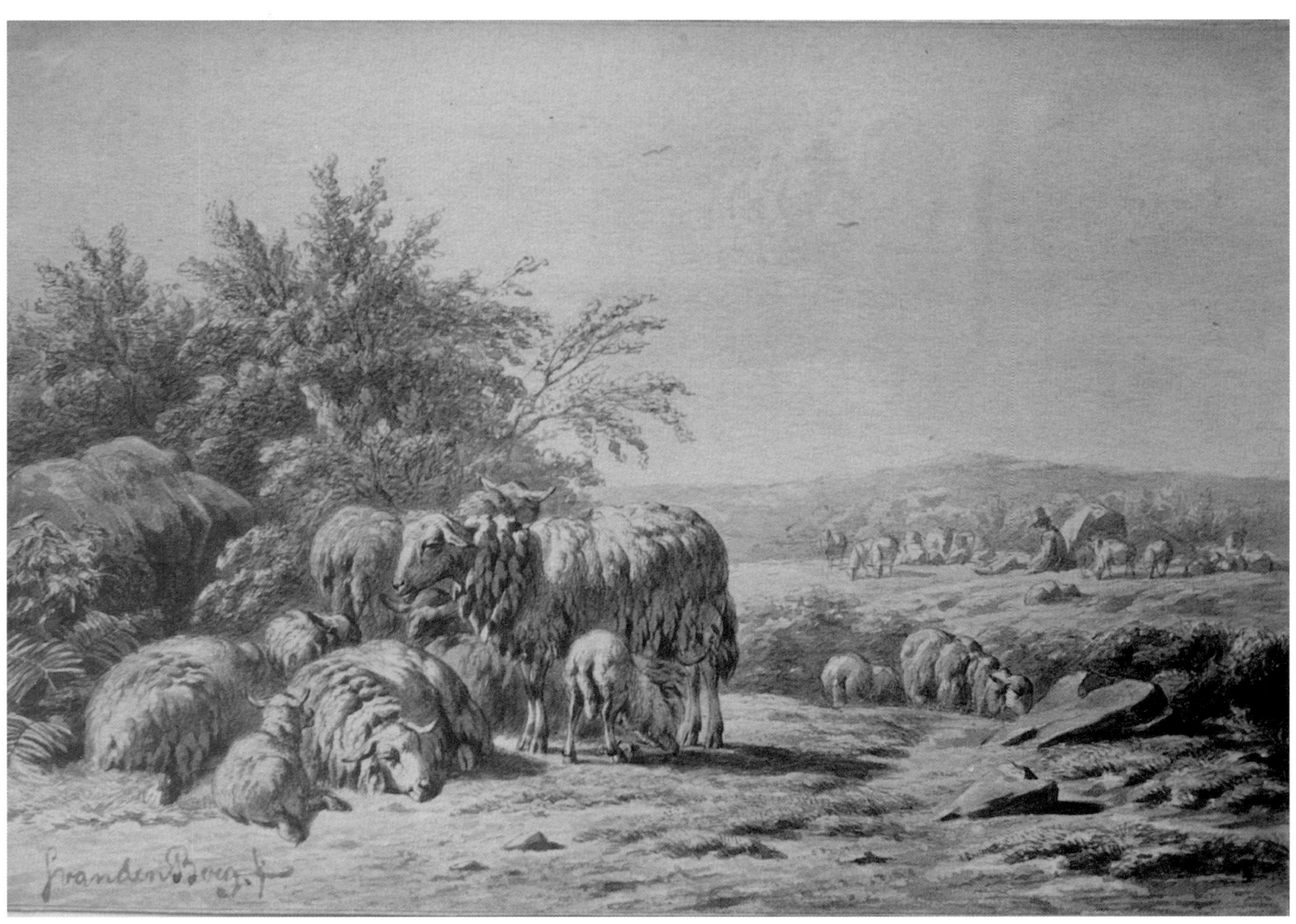

David Joseph Bles

The Hague 1821–1899 The Hague

3. *Woman with a Spinning Wheel,* 1864

Watercolor, 195 x 157 mm (7⅝ x 9⅞ in.)
Signed and dated lower left: *D. Bles. f 64*

David Joseph Bles was primarily a genre painter and The Hague's most celebrated artist during the 1850s and 1860s. He was a pupil of Cornelis Kruseman (1797–1857) at The Hague for three years, and afterwards in 1843 he studied at the studio of Robert Fleury (1797–1890) in Paris. Later he traveled to Belgium and England. He was a contemporary of Willem Roelofs (cat. 26) and Johannes Bosboom (cat. 4) with whom he helped to establish the Pulchri Studio in The Hague.[1]

Attractive women, cozy domestic scenes, humor, and double-entendre characterize his works, which were highly sought after by his middle-class patrons. His small anecdotal paintings of middle-class moral life secured his reputation to the extent that reputedly even Jozef Israëls (cat. 13) felt privileged to walk around an exhibition arm in arm with Bles.[2] He also painted larger pictures based on literary subjects. In nearly all instances his figures are attired in historical dress. The Gemeentemuseum at The Hague possesses a significant collection of his drawings and watercolors.

The subject of a woman spinning can be linked to seventeenth-century genre works that emphasized a woman's domestic responsibility and virtue. Such themes continued to be popular well into the nineteenth century. In this work Bles shows the well-dressed woman spinning with one hand at her wheel while resting her head on the other hand to produce a reflective mood. Bles was especially adept at creating a fleeting moment of charmed intimacy in his drawings.

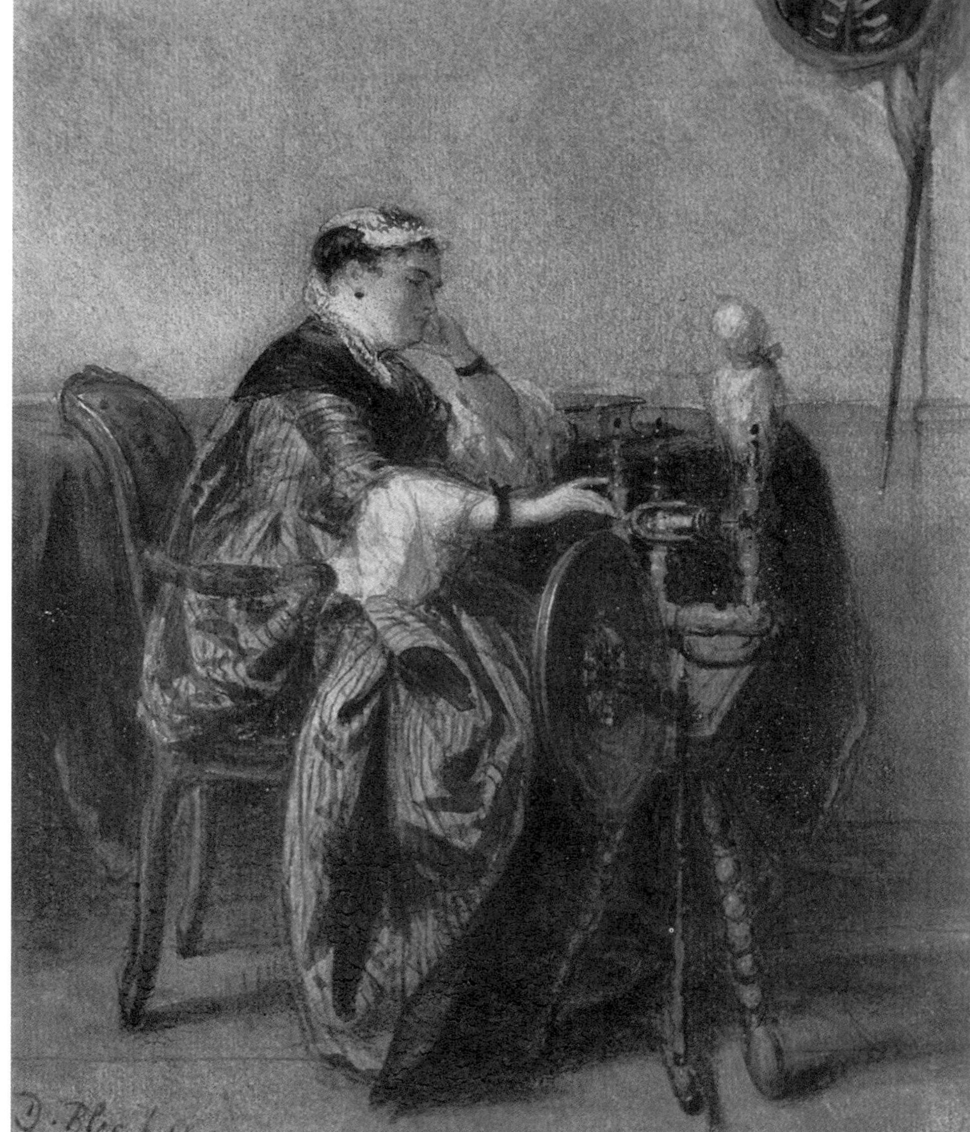

Plate I

Notes
1. De Bodt, pp. 25–40.
2. Marius, p. 93.

Johannes Bosboom

The Hague 1817–1891 The Hague

4. *Interior of Saint Laurenskerk, Rotterdam*

Watercolor, 338 x 433 mm (13¼ x 17 in.)
Signed lower left: *J Bosboom*

Johannes Bosboom primarily depicted church interiors as well as landscapes and views of historic towns. He studied at The Hague Academy under Bartholomeus Johannes van Hove (1790–1880) and was greatly influenced by the French Romantic artists. One of his fellow pupils was Samuel Verveer (cat. 33), with whom he made a study trip to Germany via Utrecht. His early drawings are from sketchbooks he kept during his travels in Holland and abroad in Germany, Belgium, and France. Bosboom was especially interested in sketching architectural monuments and sacred buildings, and from the mid-1830s paintings and drawings of church interiors—inspired by the Dutch Golden Age—were among his specialties. His subject matter also included cloisters and synagogues. He became a member of the Royal Academy in Amsterdam in 1845, and he was made a knight of the Order of Leopold in 1851. Later in his career, Bosboom began to develop watercolor as a medium in its own right and produced innumerable works of high quality, many reflecting his admiration for Rembrandt (1606–1669). Major collections of his drawings and watercolors are in the Rijksmuseum at Amsterdam, the Rijksmuseum Kröller Müller at Otterlo, and the Gemeentemuseum at The Hague.

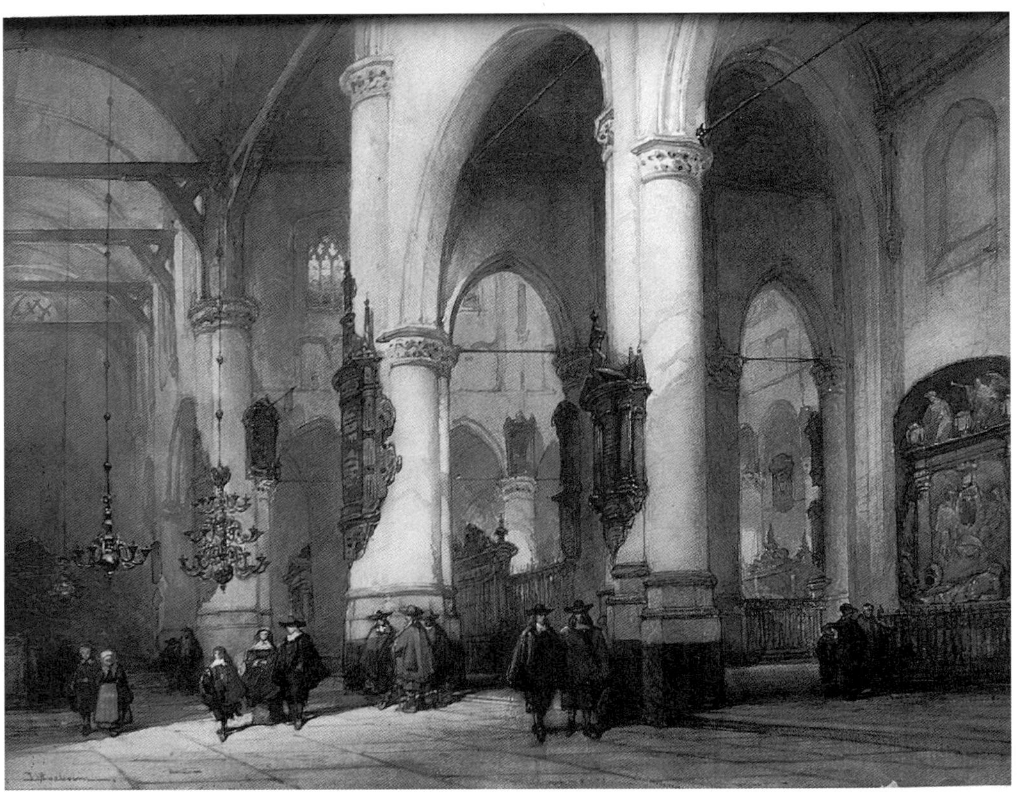

Plate II

Bosboom's drawing of the interior of Saint Laurenskerk (or Grotekerk) in Rotterdam reveals his debt to the artists of the seventeenth century who developed this genre of art. He has admirably captured the space of this late-Gothic structure built in the fifteenth century with its cruciform basilica, high wide aisles, and painted wooden barrel vaulting. Figures dressed in seventeenth-century attire add a historical note. The tomb of the navel hero Egbert M. Kortenaer (died 1665), which lies on the north side of the choir, is carefully observed and shown at the far right. Bosboom depicted this church several times, including a watercolor in a private collection in Toronto (about 1855–58) and another with a different arrangement in the print room of the Rijksmuseum in Amsterdam (no. A2550). A painted version is in the Museum Boymans-van Beuningen at Rotterdam (no. 1077).[1]

Note
1. Hurdalek, p. 30, no. 8.

Anton [Anthonie] Braakman

Rotterdam 1811–1870 Stuttgart

5. *Winter Scene*

Pen and ink and brown and gray wash, 242 x 335 mm (9⅜ x 13 in.)
Signed lower left: *A Braackman f*

Anton Braakman lived and worked in Rotterdam. In 1831 he traveled to Bremen in Germany where he remained for about one and one-half years. Four years later he was again abroad in Germany, France, and Italy. In 1844 he lived in Frankfurt and in the same year traveled through Germany, France, Belgium, and Italy. He was a pupil of Andreas Schelfhout (cat. 28). His oeuvre consists primarily of winter and summer landscapes. Braakman's work is also found in the Rijksmuseum Kröller Müller at Otterlo.

This winter scene reflects some of the preferred subject matter of the pupils of Schelfhout, who produced many watercolors and drawings of the various seasons in the Dutch Romantic mode. Braakman's *Winter Scene* with bare trees and snow-covered ground serves as the setting for such seasonal activities as skaters enjoying the pleasures afforded by the frozen canal.

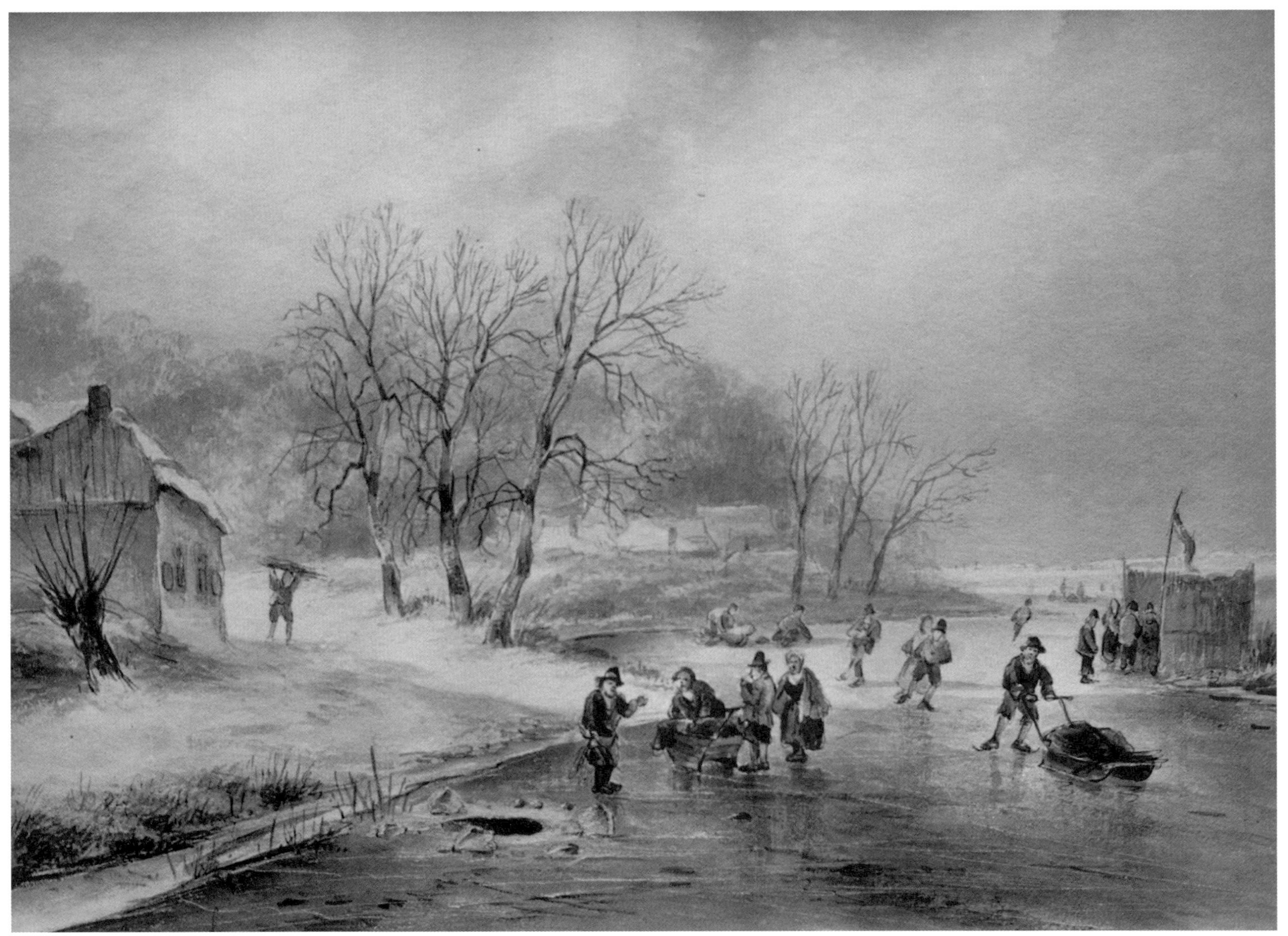

Hendrik Gerrit ten Cate

Amsterdam 1803–1856 Amsterdam

6. *Landscape with Cows,* 1836

Pen and brown ink and watercolor, 110 x 133 mm (4¼ x 5¼ in.)
Signed and dated lower left: *H G ten Cate 1836*

Hendrik Gerrit ten Cate lived and worked in Amsterdam where he was a pupil of Pieter George Westenberg (1791–1873). He painted portraits, landscapes, fruit and flower still lifes, and later city views illuminated by moonlight. He is especially remembered for his drawings in color and those in East India ink. Major collections of his work are in the Teylers Stichting at Haarlem, the Gemeentemuseum at The Hague, the Gemeentearchief at Amsterdam, and the Museum Boymans-van Beuningen at Rotterdam.

In this drawing Ten Cate, who is dependent on subject matter treated by seventeenth-century artists, captures the flatness of the Dutch countryside with its low horizon and cloudy sky through the careful control of horizontal and vertical lines. The treatment of the gate and cows in the foreground with reflections of light and shadow on the canal contrasts effectively with the more lightly drawn distant scene, creating a serene atmosphere.

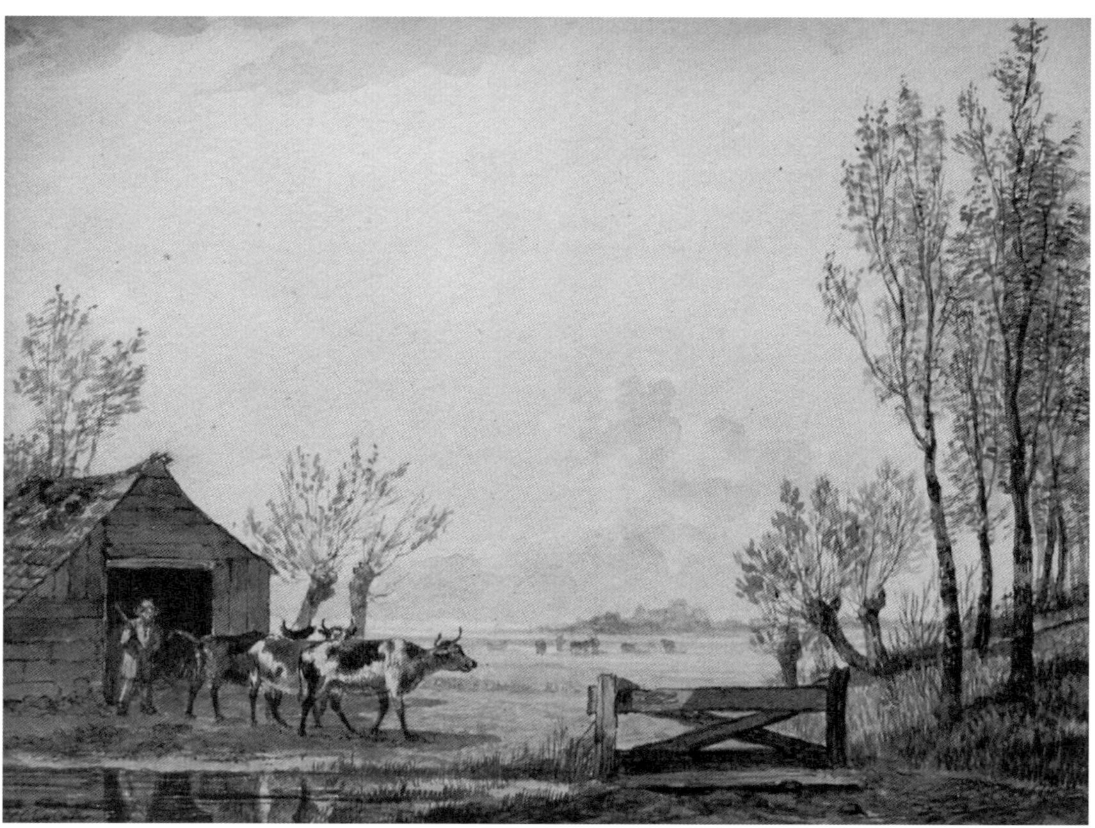

Plate III

Willem Cornelis van Dijk

Utrecht 1826–1881 Amsterdam

7. *Alphabet Lesson*

Watercolor and black and colored chalks, 265 x 302 mm (10⅜ x 11⅞ in.)
Signed upper right: *Willem van Dijk*

Willem Cornelis van Dijk produced many paintings, drawings, and etchings of genre and interior scenes. He worked mainly in Utrecht until 1870 when he moved to Amsterdam. The Gemeentearchief at Utrecht has a large number of his drawings.

The Dutch have always put a high premium on the importance of religious, intellectual, and moral education for a virtuous life.[1] Essential in this equation is proper child rearing (see also cat. 10). Since the seventeenth century the loci for training children included the church and the school although in reality this task frequently occurred in the home. Van Dijk's watercolor, which shows a teacher and three children engaged in the learning process, pays homage to the school genre as developed during

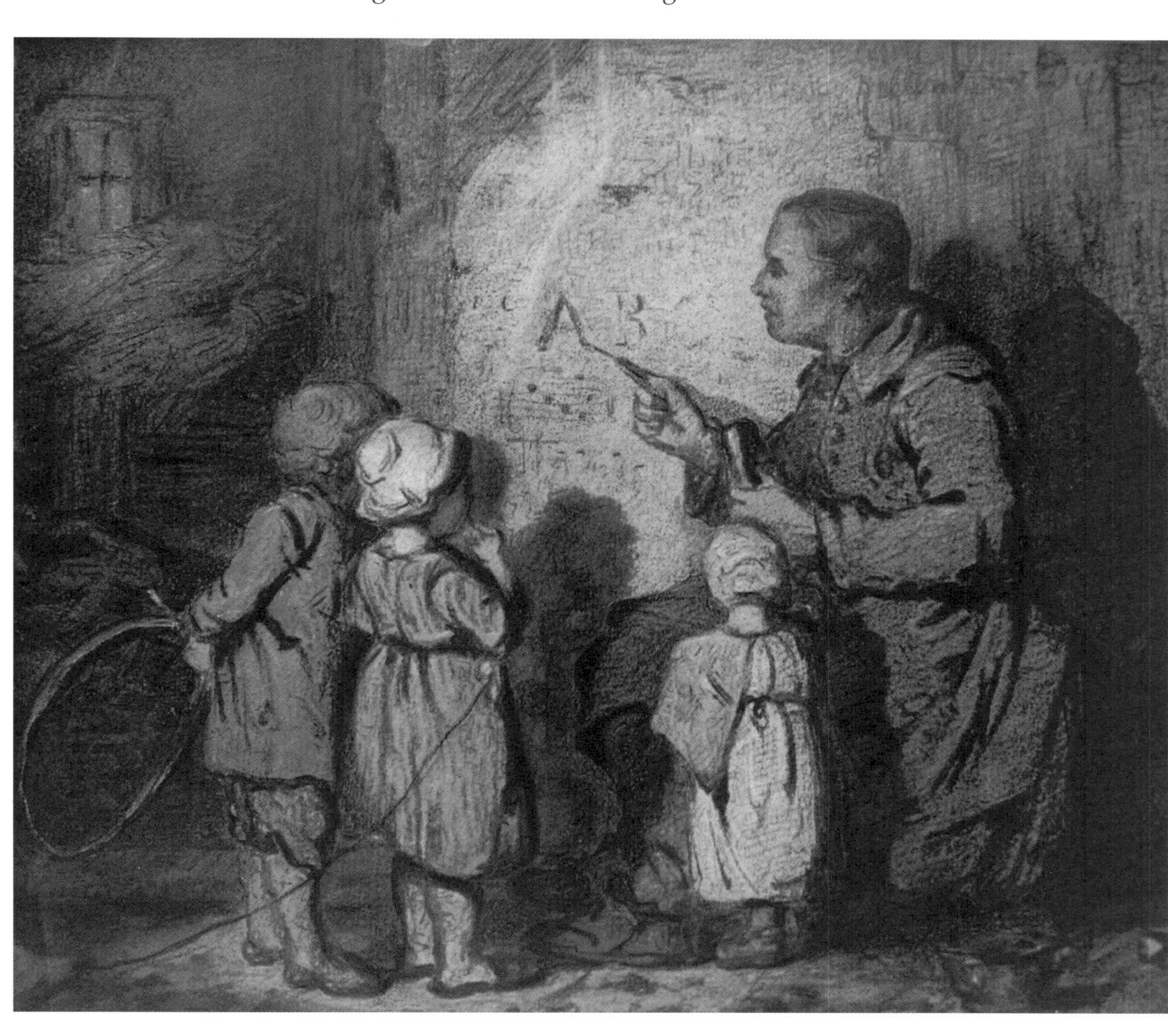

Plate IV

the Dutch Golden Age. Both the alphabet and musical citations are indicated on the wall. The small boy at the left is on his best behavior, attending to the lesson rather than playing with his hoop, a child's toy frequently shown in Dutch art.

Note
1. Franits, pp. 111–60.

Allaert van Everdingen

Alkmaar 1621–1675 Amsterdam

8. *Landscape with Sheep*

Pen and brown ink and wash over traces of black chalk, 157 x 209 mm (6⅛ x 8¼ in.)

Allaert van Everdingen was a painter and engraver of seascapes and rugged Scandinavian landscapes. His oeuvre comprises about 1600 paintings, 166 etchings, one mezzotint, and more than 600 drawings.[1] He was a pupil of Roelandt Savery (1576?–1639) at Utrecht and later of Peter Molijn (cat. 22) at Haarlem. He traveled in Sweden and Norway from 1640 to 1644. When he returned, he introduced the Scandinavian landscape of pine forests, craggy cliffs, and waterfalls to Dutch art. Van Everdingen's work influenced Jacob van Ruisdael (1628/29–1682), the great seventeenth-century landscape artist. His drawings are found in both public and private collections throughout Europe and the United States.

Everdingen's drawings treat a much broader range of themes than his paintings and include rivers, marines, villages, coastlines, and farms. Most of them are finished compositions signed with his monogram and were probably made for sale.[2] This work is characteristic of the realistic phase of seventeenth-century Dutch landscape art with the tonal modulation of the land receding to the horizon dominated by a high sky. The use of light and washes animates the figures and animals in the foreground.

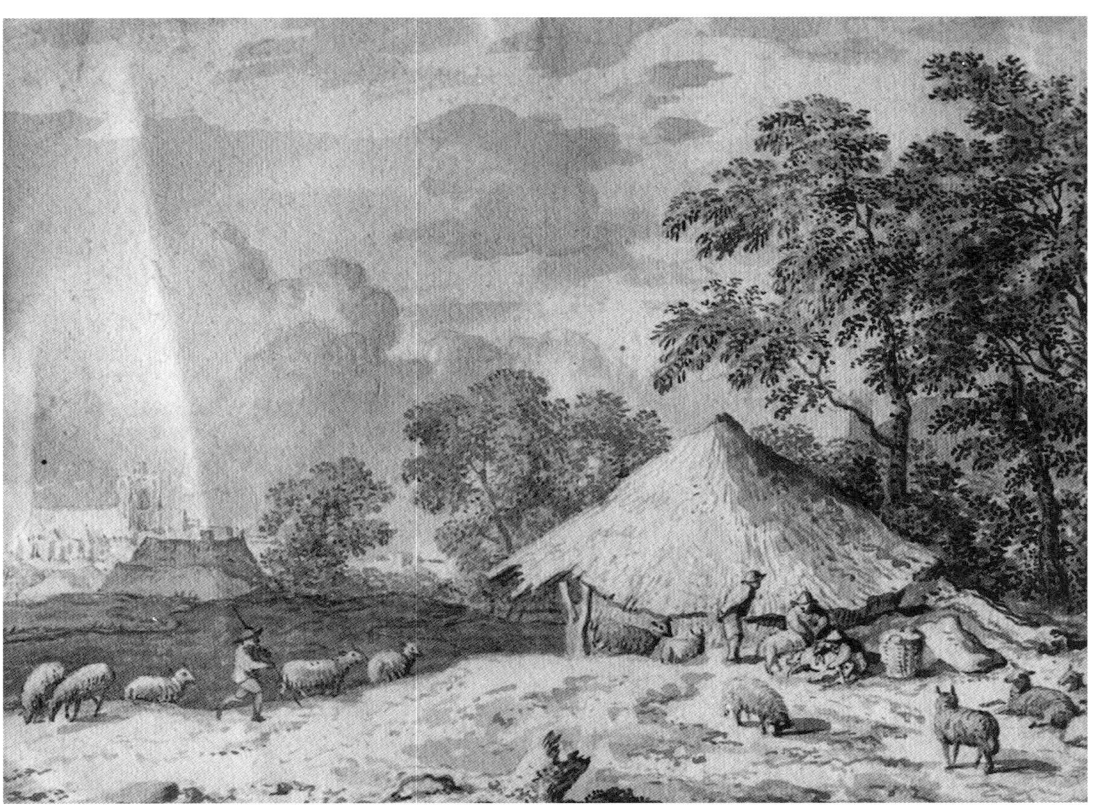

Notes
1. Davies, pp. 3–4
2. Robinson, in Robinson and Schatborn, p. 96.

9. *River Landscape with a Boat*

Pen and brown ink and wash, 105 x 101 mm (4⅛ x 4 in.)
Signed lower left: *AVE*

In the 1650s Everdingen produced a number of river scenes dependent on a type of diagonal composition developed by Esaias van de Velde (about 1590–1630), Jan van Goyen (1596–1656), and Salomon van Ruysdael (about 1602–1670) in the 1620s and 1630s.[1] Unlike many of his works that are characterized by lively activity, this drawing is a much more peaceful scene of a single boat moving on the river.

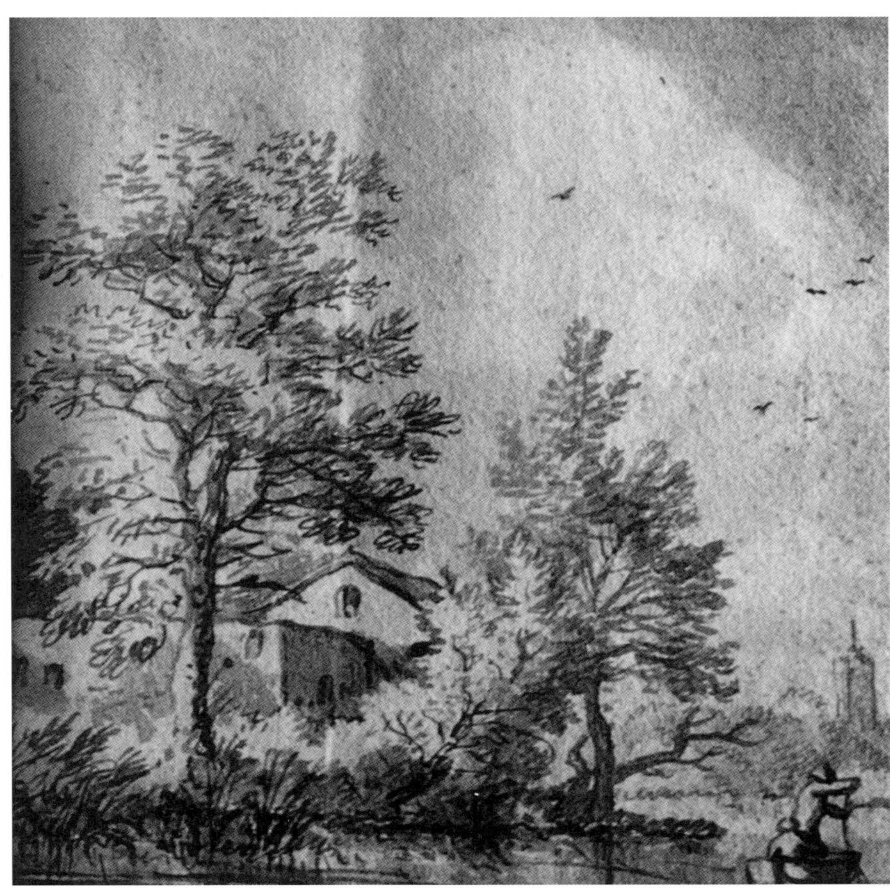

Note
1. Robinson, in Robinson and Schatborn, p. 96.

Sas van Gent 1822–1907 The Hague

10. *Woman by a Cradle*

Watercolor, 330 x 267 mm (13 x 10½ in.)
Signed lower right: *von Franckenberg*

Desirée Oscar Léopold von Franckenberg en Proschlitz worked at The Hague Academy during 1849–50 and also studied with Willem Hendrik Schmidt (1809–1849) in Delft. Later he lived and worked at The Hague where he was one of the members of the Pulchri Studio. He mostly painted beautifully clothed women in intimate interior scenes or social gatherings and also made lithographs. Most of his works are in Russian collections.

Hundreds of images from the seventeenth century depict mothers and to a lesser extent fathers involved with child rearing, attesting to the significance of childhood and the importance of molding good behavior in children so that they would become moral and virtuous adults.[1] Seventeenth-century writers established an ideal vision of child rearing that would not have been put into practice uniformly throughout the Dutch nation but that emphasized the importance of this parental responsibility. This work harks back to those seventeenth-century genre pictures that depict maternal tasks of women feeding their children or placing them in cradles. Within the somewhat stark yet neatly defined room, the mother has risen from her chair to look longingly at her child asleep in the cradle, creating a tender mood.

Note
1. Franits, pp. 111–22.

Holland, seventeenth century

11. *On the Ice*

Black chalk and gray wash, 160 x 258 mm (6⅜ x 10⅛ in.)

Jan van Goyen (1596–1656), one of the more important Dutch landscape painters before Jacob van Ruisdael (1628/29–1682), was a pupil of Esaias van de Velde (about 1590–1630) and a prolific draftsman. Most of his drawings—winter scenes, beaches, markets, dunes, seascapes, and rivers—were finished compositions intended for sale and bear his monogram, *VG*, and a date. They were generally executed in black chalk in the 1630s and early 1640s, and from 1647 he sparingly applied gray or brown wash for shadows and tone. He was particularly successful in rendering the effects of sunlight on water.[1]

Although this winter landscape with figures engaged in various activities on ice—including skating and golf—was a subject Van Goyen treated several times, especially in the 1650s, the lack of monogram and date poses questions about authenticity. According to the art historian Hans-Ulrich Beck, the Kharkiv work is by an unknown follower but not a copy after a known drawing.[2]

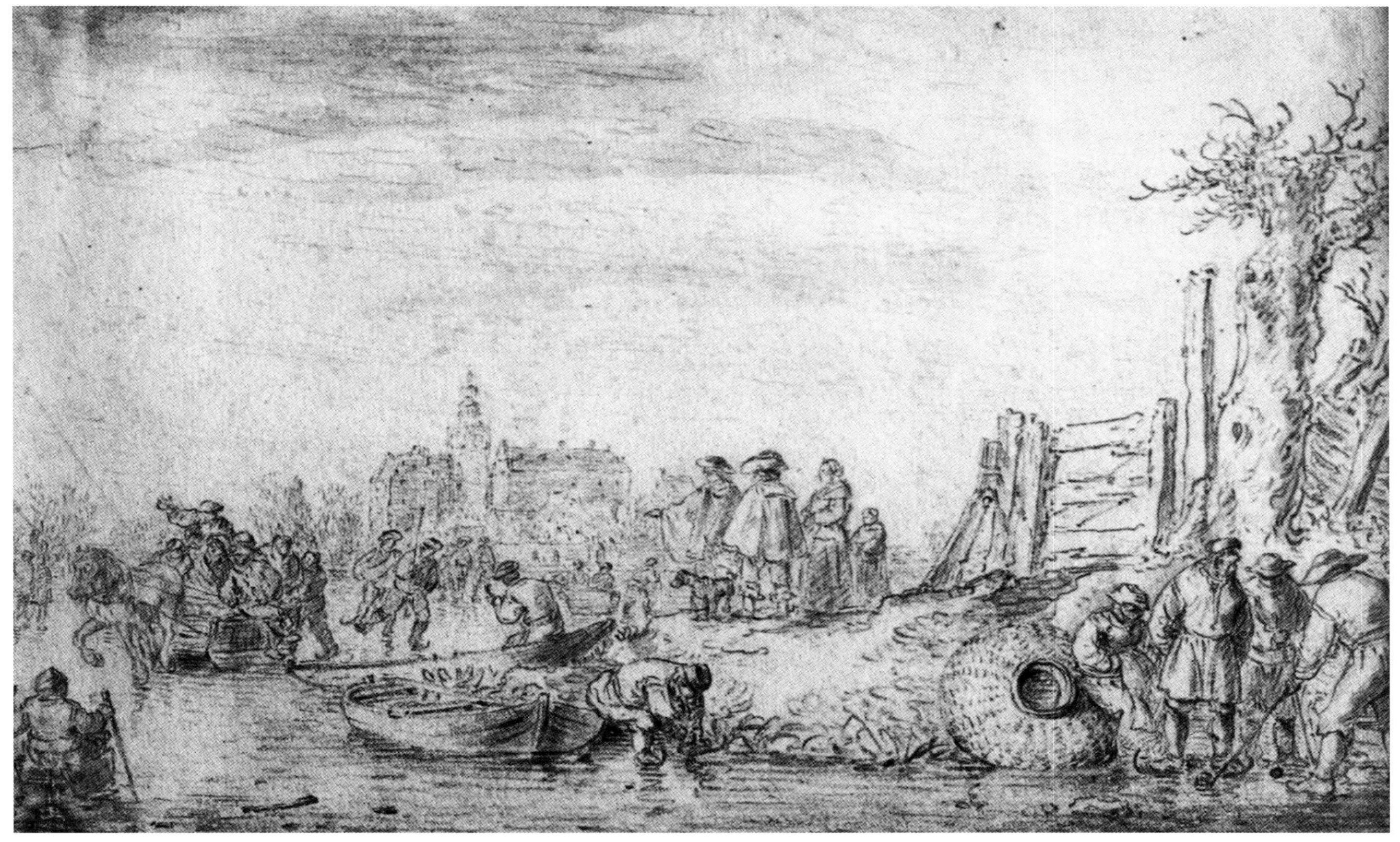

Notes

1. Beck I, pp. 51–53.

2. Beck, letter to the author, 11 Jan. 1996. For comparison see Beck I, nos. 335–57, and Beck III, nos. 195, 341, 348, and 353.

The Hague 1819–1866 The Hague

12. *Autumn Landscape,* 1862

Watercolor, 358 x 268 mm (14 x 10½ in.)
Signed and dated lower left: *J.F. Hoppenbrouwers. ft.62*

Jan Frans Hoppenbrouwers was chiefly a landscape painter of winter and summer scenes. He was a pupil at The Hague Academy and later studied with Andreas Schelfhout (cat. 28); he became a member of the Royal Academy in Amsterdam in 1845. He gave lessons to Louis Apol (1850–1936) and Antonius Josephus Madlener (1827–1890). The figures in his pictures have been painted by Schelfhout, David Joseph Bles (cat. 3), Petrus Gerardus Vertin (cat. 31), and Samuel Verveer (cat. 33). He also made etchings and lithographs. Significant collections of his drawings and watercolors are in the Rijksprentenkabinet at Amsterdam, the Rijksprentenkabinet at Leiden, and the Gemeentearchief at Haarlem.

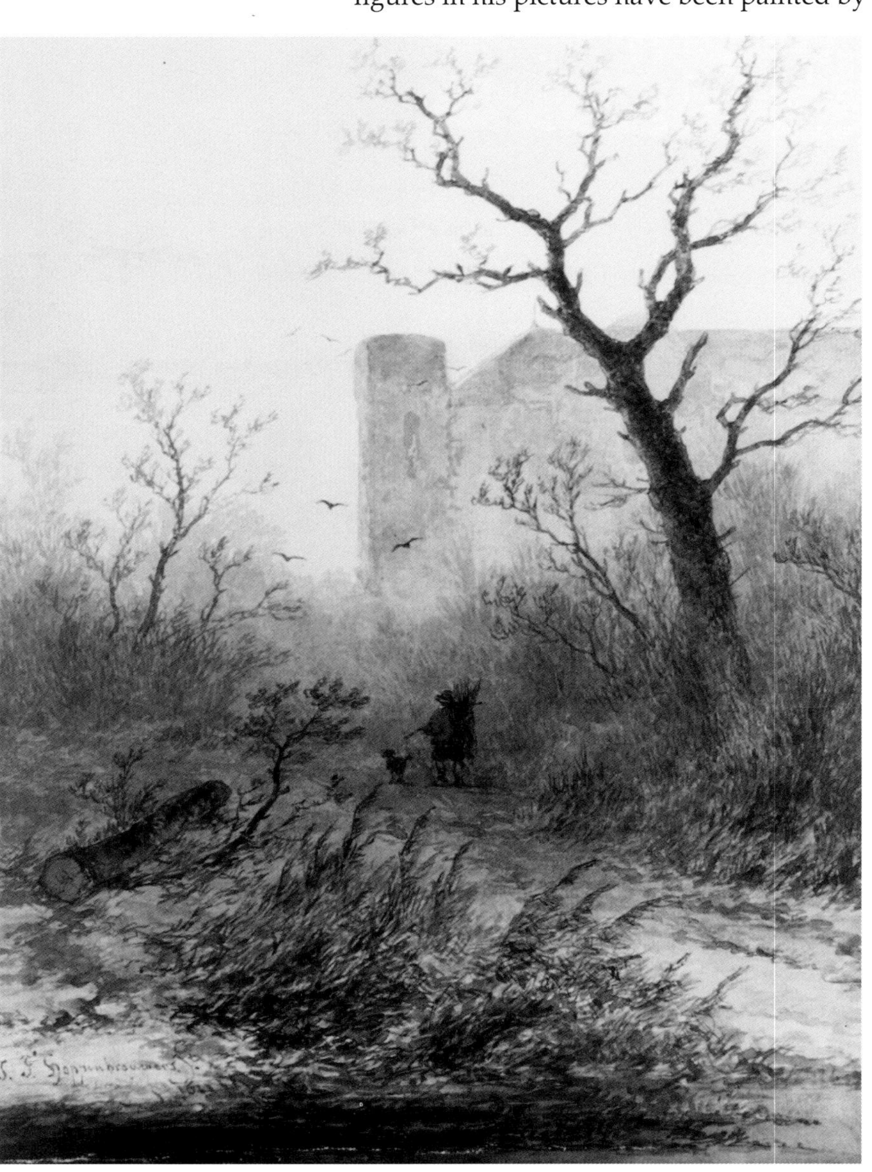

Hoppenbrouwers produced several watercolor drawings of landscapes. He liked the motif of the figure seen from behind—especially a hunter, shepherd, or traveler—placed in the middle ground. Particularly effective in this watercolor is the handling of the grasses, trees, and atmospheric color to create a mood appropriate for a fall landscape. Like many of the artists who worked in the Dutch Romantic period, Hoppenbrouwers preferred to make drawings that depicted different seasons for their emotional content: a winter landscape signed and dated 1860 was at one time with the Rococo Art Dealers,[1] and a farm in a stormy landscape dated 1863 has appeared on the art market at various times.[2]

Notes

1. Photograph, Rijksbureau voor Kunsthistorische Documentatie (RKD), The Hague.

2. Sale, London (Sotheby's; photograph RKD); Sale, Amsterdam (Christie's), 14 June 1994, no. 93, from a collection at Heilo.

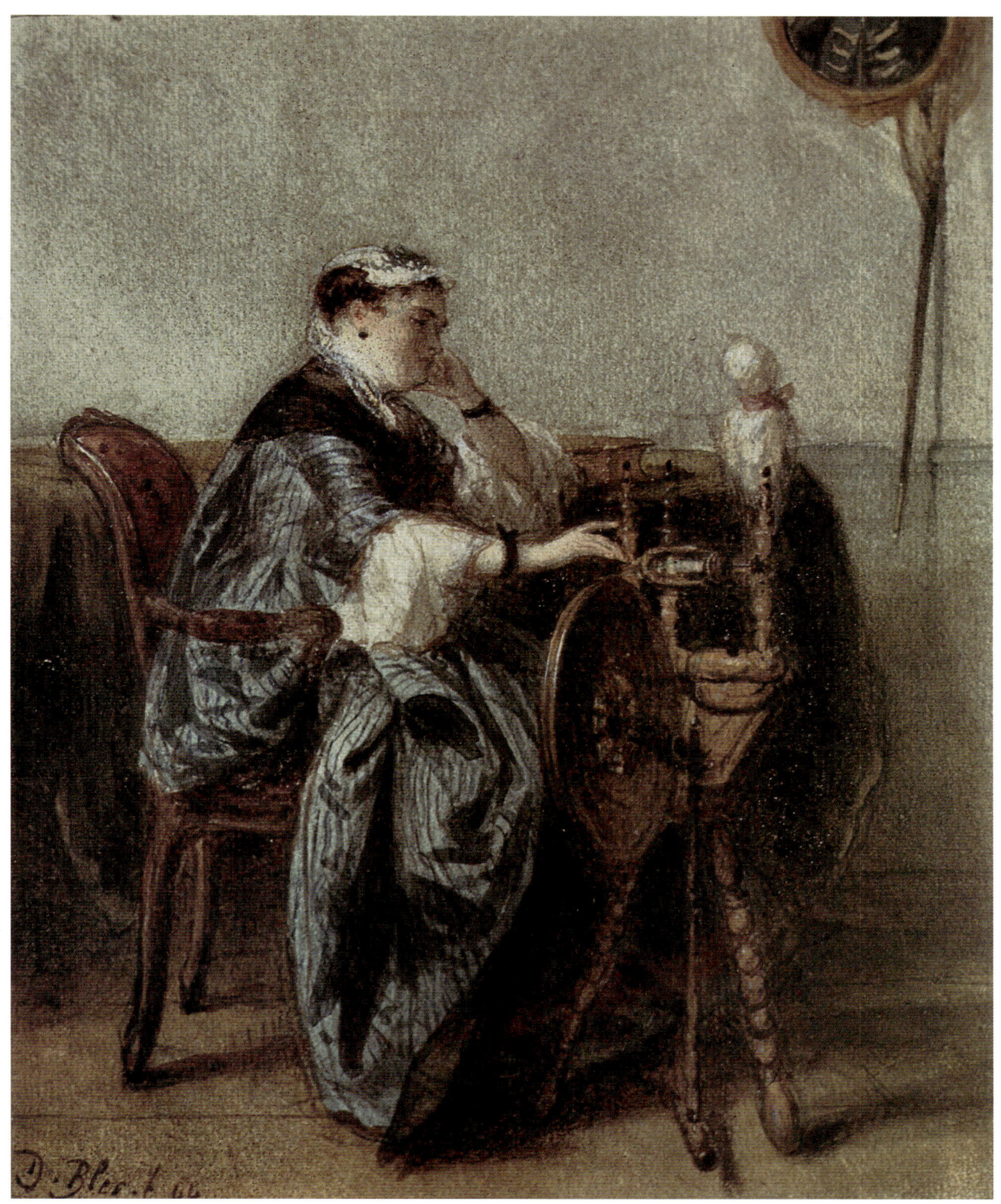

Plate I
David Joseph Bles (1821–1899)
Woman with a Spinning Wheel, 1864
Watercolor, 195 x 157 mm
Catalogue 3

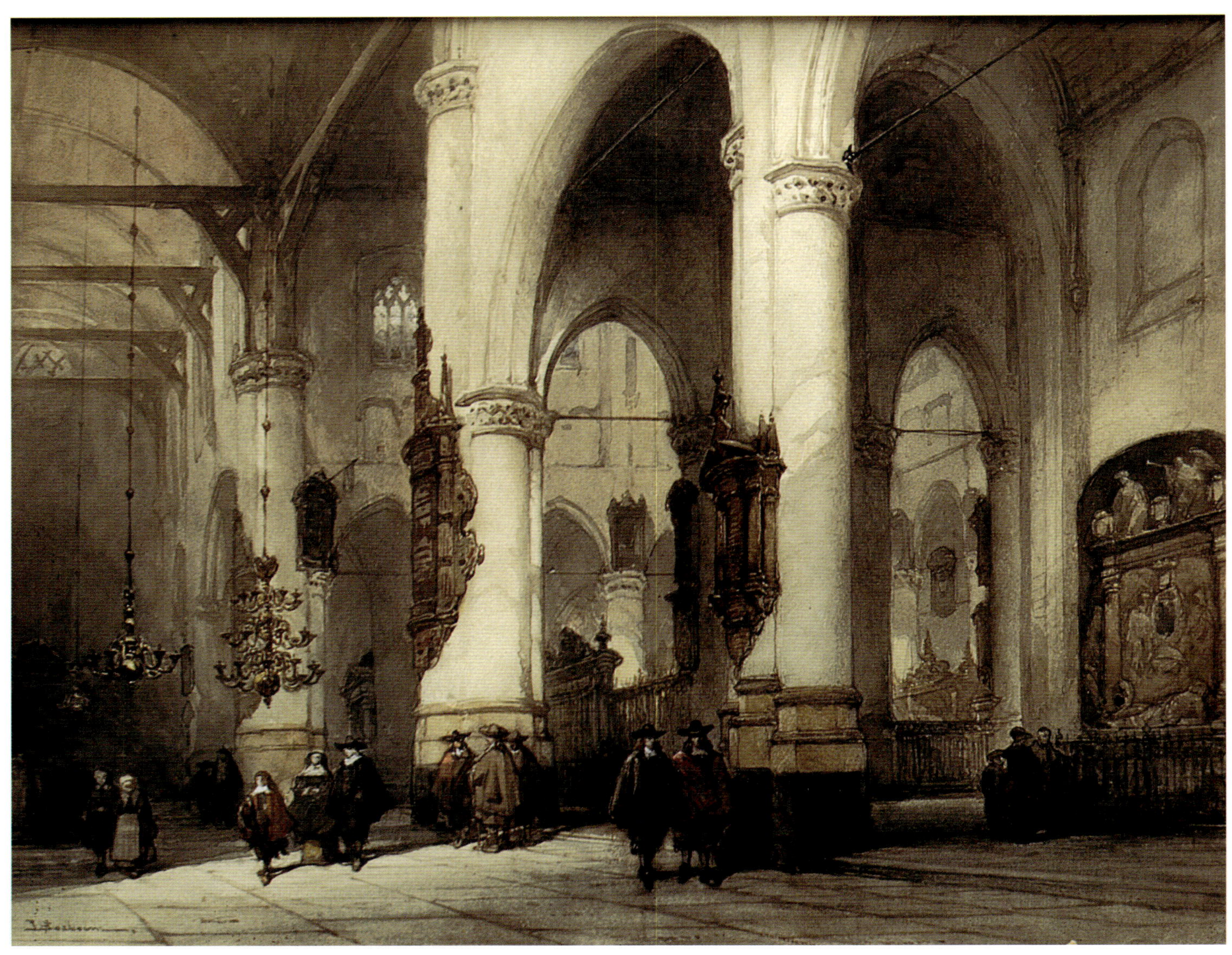

Plate II
Johannes Bosboom (1817–1891)
Interior of Saint Laurenskerk, Rotterdam
Watercolor, 338 x 433 mm
Catalogue 4

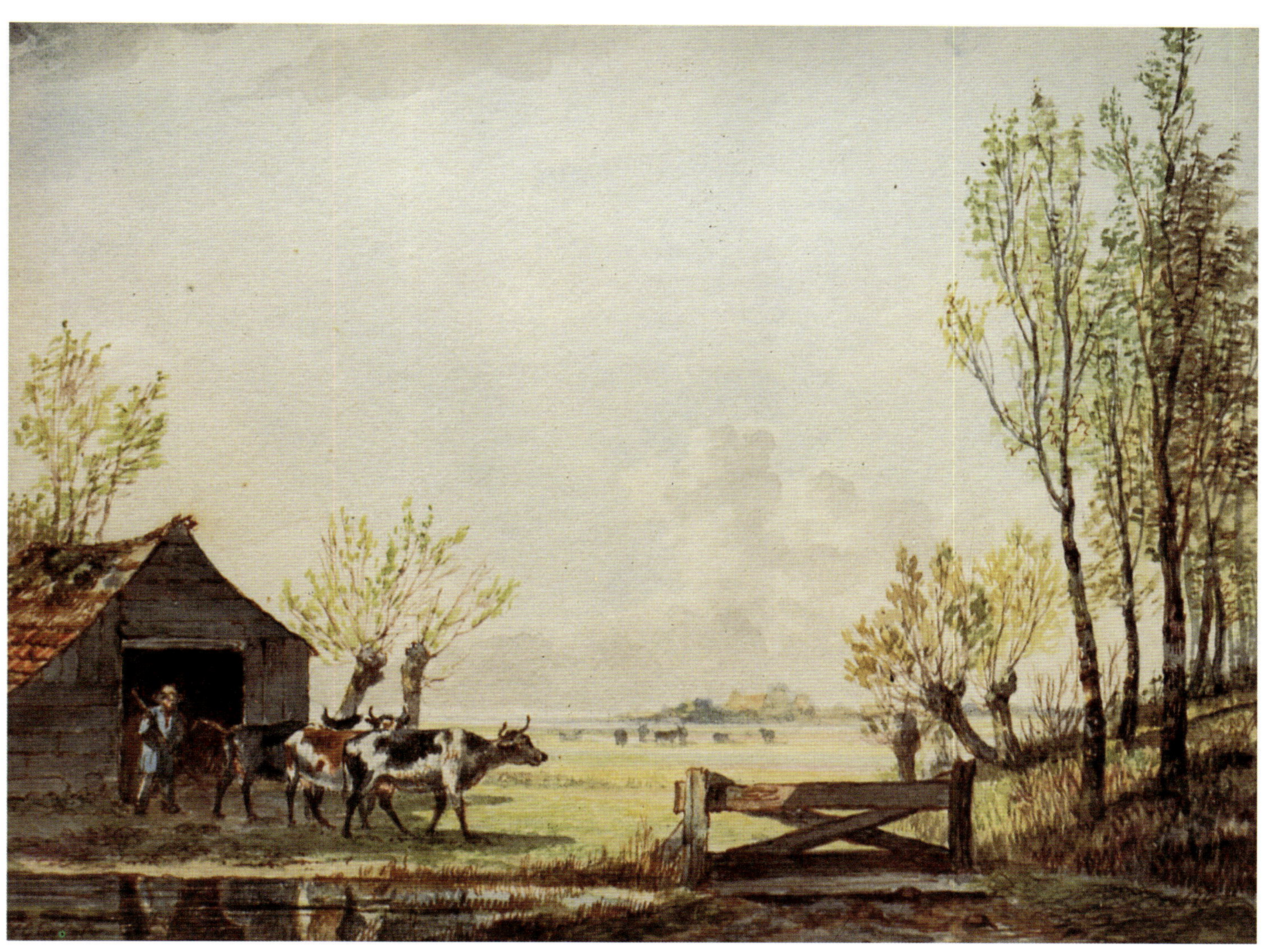

Plate III
Hendrick Gerrit ten Cate (1803–1856)
Landscape with Cows, 1836
Pen and brown ink and watercolor, 110 x 133 mm
Catalogue 6

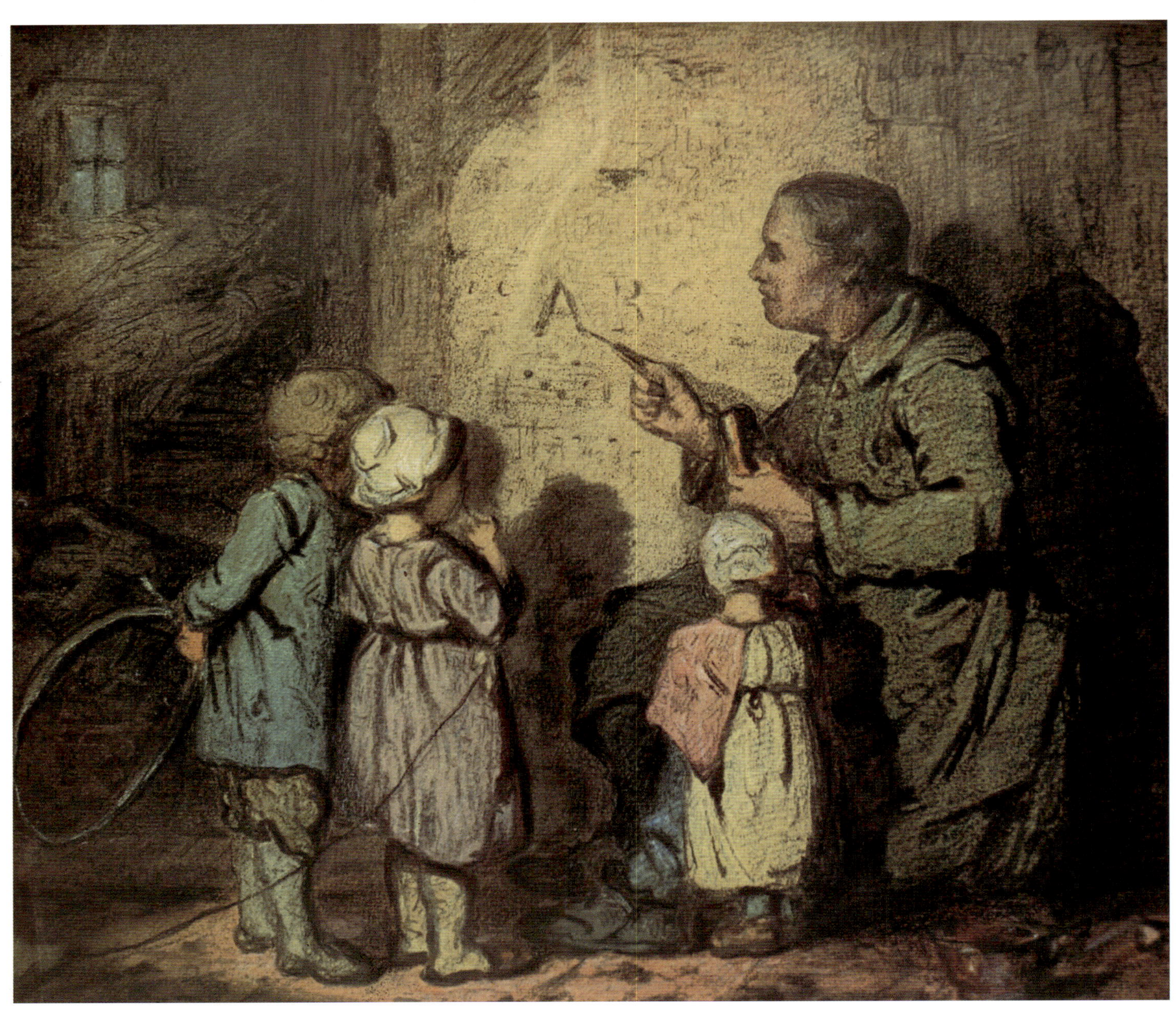

Plate IV
Willem Cornelis van Dijk (1826–1881)
Alphabet Lesson
Watercolor and black and colored chalks, 265 x 302 mm
Catalogue 7

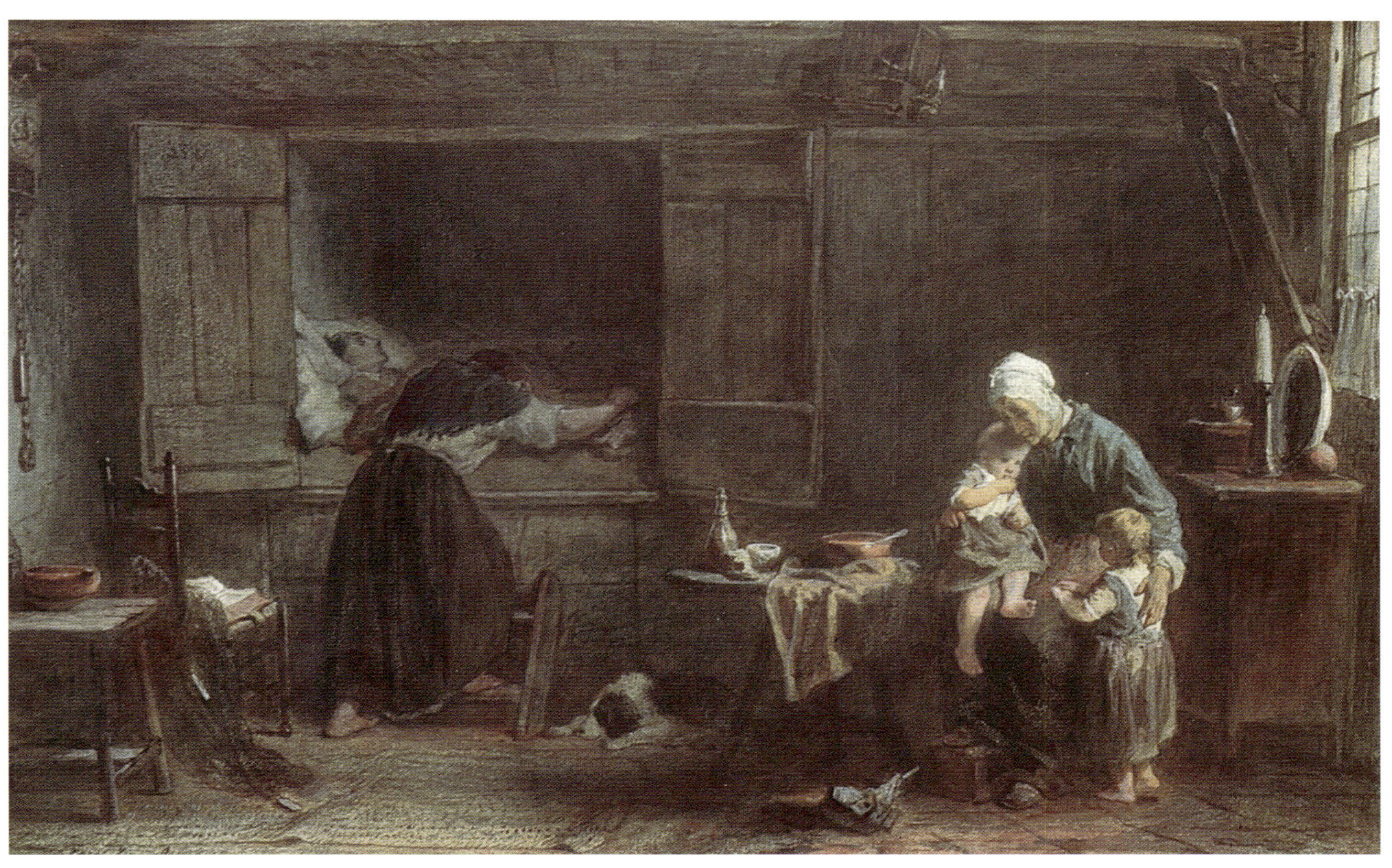

Plate V
Jozef Israëls (1824–1911)
Fisherman's Death
Watercolor, 295 x 470 mm
Catalogue 13

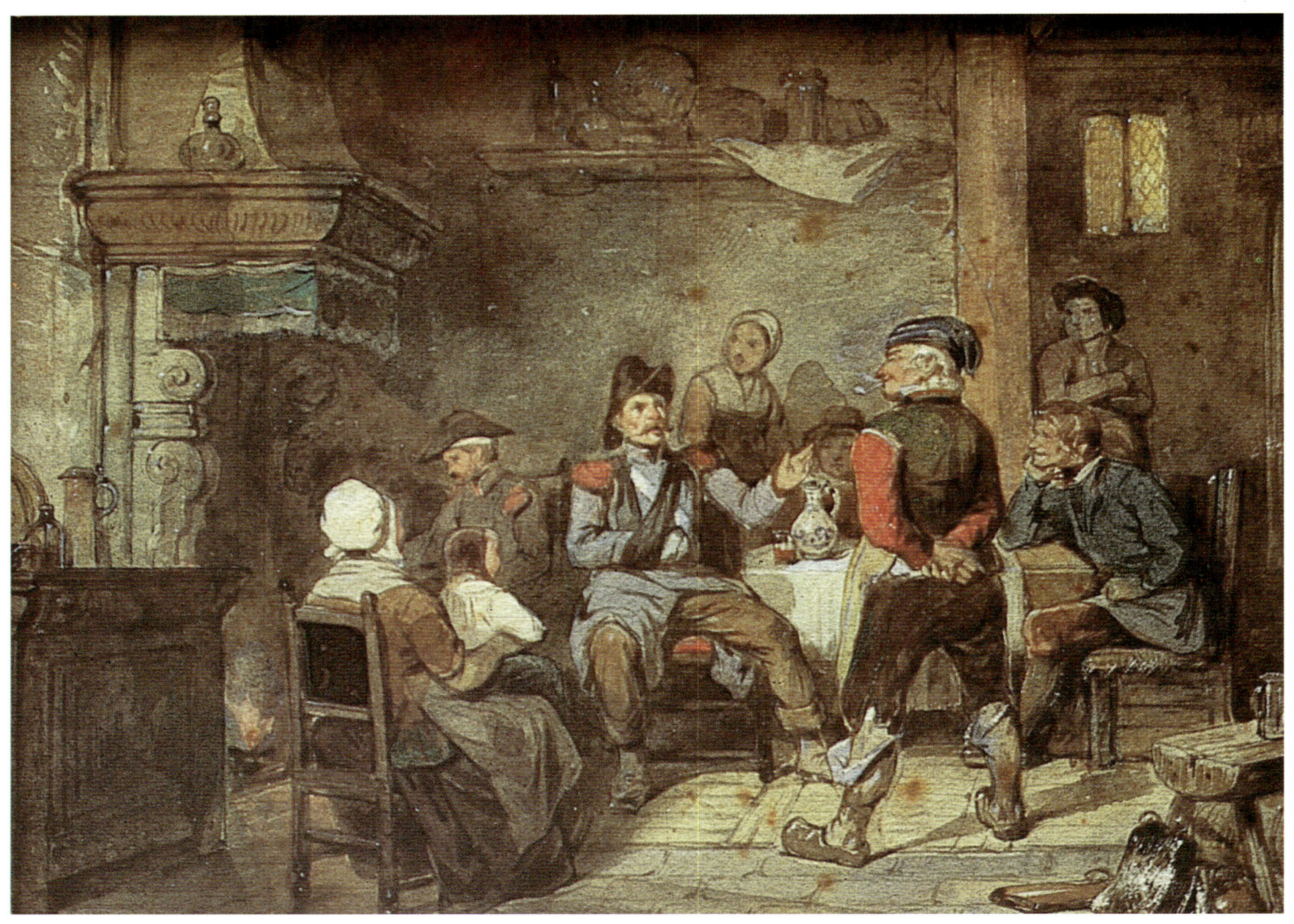

Plate VI
Herman Frederik Carel ten Kate (1822–1891)
Soldier's Story
Watercolor, 148 x 201 mm
Catalogue 14

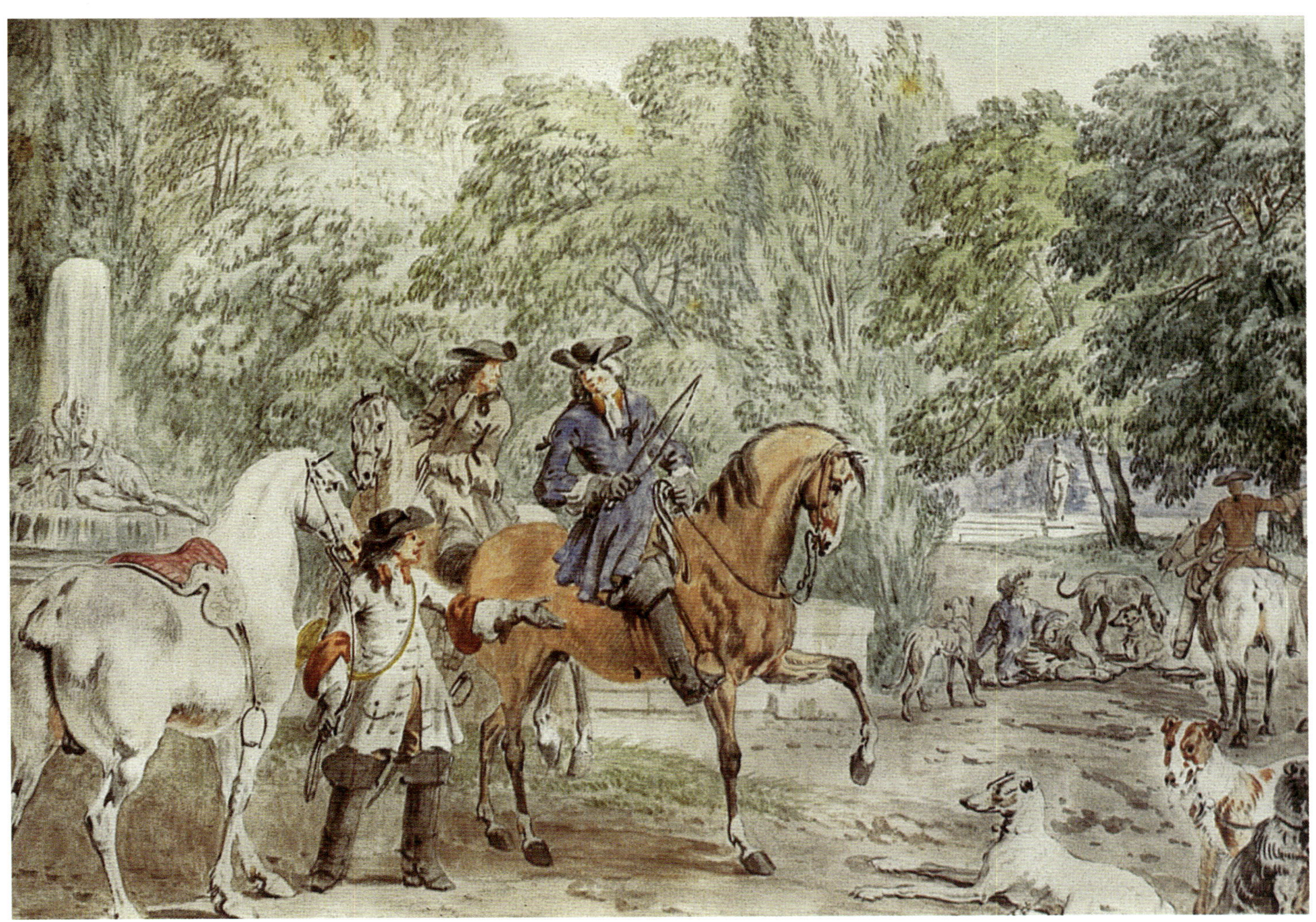

Plate VII
Dirk Maes (1659–1717)
Hunters
Watercolor, 170 x 252 mm
Catalogue 20

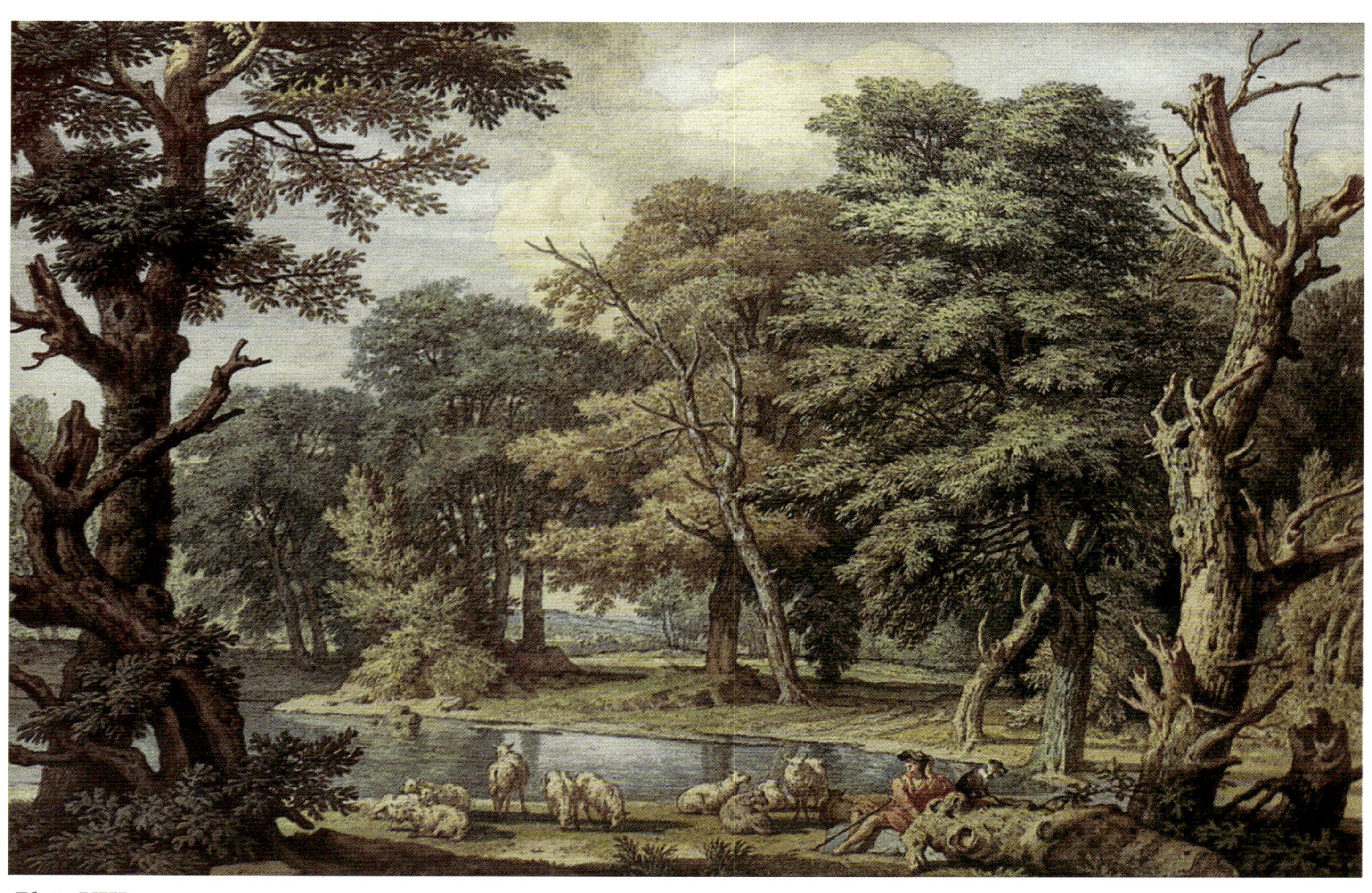

Plate VIII
Isaac de Moucheron (1667–1744)
Forest Landscape, 1738
Black chalk and watercolor, 230 x 343 mm
Catalogue 23

Jozef Israëls

Groningen 1824–1911 The Hague

13. *Fisherman's Death*

Watercolor, 295 x 470 mm (11⅝ x 18½ in.)
Signed lower left: *Jozef Israels*

Jozef Israëls specialized in the depiction of rural landscapes and the simple lives of peasants. He was born into a poor and devout Jewish family in Groningen and first studied at its Minerva Academy. In 1840 he joined the studio of John Adam Kruseman (1804–1862) of Amsterdam. From 1845 to 1847 he studied in Paris, where at the Louvre he copied and studied the works of Rembrandt van Rijn (1606–1669) and Diego Velázquez (1599–1660), who influenced his work. During the early 1850s he traveled to the Barbizon region of France, where he drew peasant interiors and bought peasant clothing. About 1854 he began to paint scenes of the seacoast and the lives of fisherfolk, for which he is well known. This subject was already popular in literature in Europe before mid-century. Israëls was especially attracted to the villages of Katwijk and Scheveningen on the Dutch coast, where he was struck by

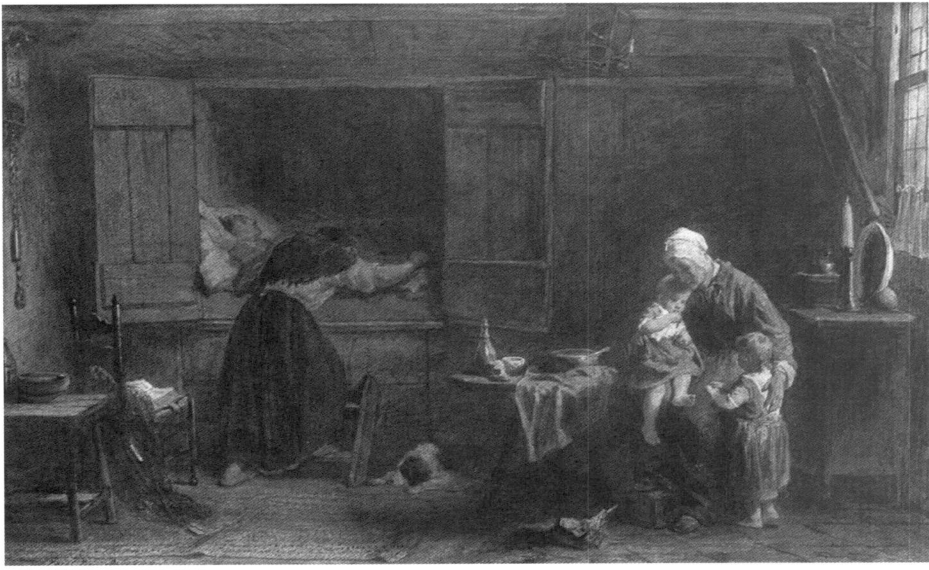

Plate V

the beauty of the beach and the simple but noble lives of the people.[1] Fishing communities and aspects of Jewish life remained his primary subject matter throughout his life. In 1869 he settled with his family in The Hague and soon became a leading figure in the group of artists known as the Hague School. He influenced many later Dutch and German painters. When he died, he was recognized as one of the leaders of modern Dutch art. Major collections of his drawings are in the Stedelijk Museum at Amsterdam, the Gemeentemuseum at The Hague, and the Rijksmuseum Kröller Müller at Otterlo.

Israëls was accomplished in the art of watercolor and was a founding member of the Dutch Drawing Society, a circle of artists who promoted watercolor as an independent art form.[2] With its concentration on grief and loss, this drawing is consistent with many Israëls executed. He especially liked deathbed themes, which may have been inspired by the Dutch genre painter Petrus Marius Molijn (1819–1849).[3] In this watercolor the woman in the left background leans over the sickbed of a dying man while the woman on the right comforts two small children. In his watercolors and paintings of grieving fisherfolk, he liked to place the figures and bed parallel to the picture plane, reminiscent of neoclassical works.[4] Israëls's interest in chiaroscuro, the manner in which light and shade can be manipulated to enhance the mood of a piece, is evident in this work.

Notes

1. De Haan, in Rotterdam 1995, p. 68.

2. Sillevis, p. 12.

3. Compare Molijn's etched and painted versions of the deathbed (Knoef, pp. 120–21).

4. For example, compare the paintings *Alone in the World*, 1880, in the Mesdag Museum, The Hague (De Gruyter, pl. 65); and *Day Before Parting*, 1862, in the Museum of Fine Arts, Boston (De Leeuw, no. 30).

Herman [Frederik Carel] ten Kate

The Hague 1822–1891 The Hague

14. *Soldier's Story*
Watercolor, 148 x 201 mm (5¾ x 7⅞ in.)
Signed lower right: *H.F.C. ten Kate f.*

Herman ten Kate was a genre painter who produced pictures illustrating the Eighty Years' War. He was a pupil of Cornelis Kruseman (1797–1857) from 1837 to 1841 and later studied with Alexander Hugo Bakker Korff (1824–1882). He made trips to Belgium, Germany, Italy, and France during 1840–42, returning to The Hague where he studied at its academy. In 1847 he became a member of the Royal Academy in Amsterdam and in 1856 at Rotterdam's academy. He worked in The Hague until 1867, in Amsterdam to 1868, and in Haarlem and The Hague from 1869. His work, especially his depictions of the war, exhibit a talent for accurate depiction of detail. It has been noted, however, that the figures appear staged in their settings. He worked at a time when the French artist Jean-Louis-Ernest Meissonier (1815–1891) was in vogue, and his work was highly sought after in his lifetime.[1] He produced paintings, watercolors, and lithographs.

Herman ten Kate executed a number of drawings that depict interior settings reminiscent of tavern scenes by seventeenth-century artists such as Adriaen van Ostade (1610–1685) and Adriaen Brouwer (1606–1638). Here, the soldier with a wounded arm holds the attention of men and women alike with his story. Other works with seventeenth-century interiors are found in the Rijksmuseum at Amsterdam, the Teylers Stichting at Haarlem, and the Museum Boymans-van Beuningen at Rotterdam.

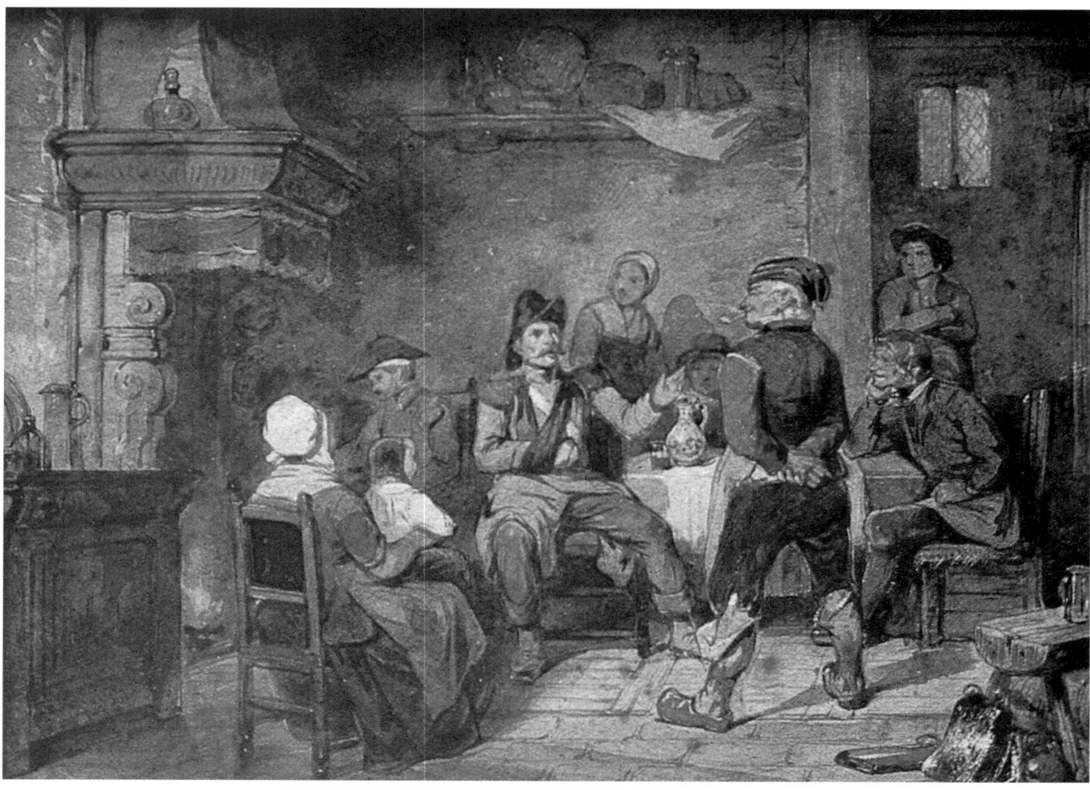

Note
1. Marius, p. 99.

Plate VI

[JOHAN] MARI [HENRI] TEN KATE

The Hague 1831–1910 Driebergen

15. *Girl by a Spring,* 1850

Watercolor, 200 x 237 mm (7⅞ x 9¼ in.)
Signed and dated lower left: *Mari ten Kate f 50*

Mari ten Kate chiefly drew and painted scenes of children. He was the younger brother and pupil of Herman ten Kate (cat. 14). He was in Amsterdam from 1850 to 1871, and in 1852 he became a member of the Royal Academy there. From 1871 to 1905 he was in The Hague, then Driebergen. He made trips to Paris, England, Italy, and the Netherlands' East Indies. His studies are considered to be of better quality than his finished paintings, and significant collections are in the Rijksprentenkabinet at Amsterdam, the Teylers Stichting at Haarlem, and the Rijksmuseum Kröller Müller at Otterlo.

Mari ten Kate generally depicted children at play. In this spirit the Kharkiv drawing shows a girl cooling her feet in a pool of water set among trees. The carefree mood of the drawing is reinforced by the handling of light and shade and by showing the young girl's basket set aside near the trunk of one of the trees.

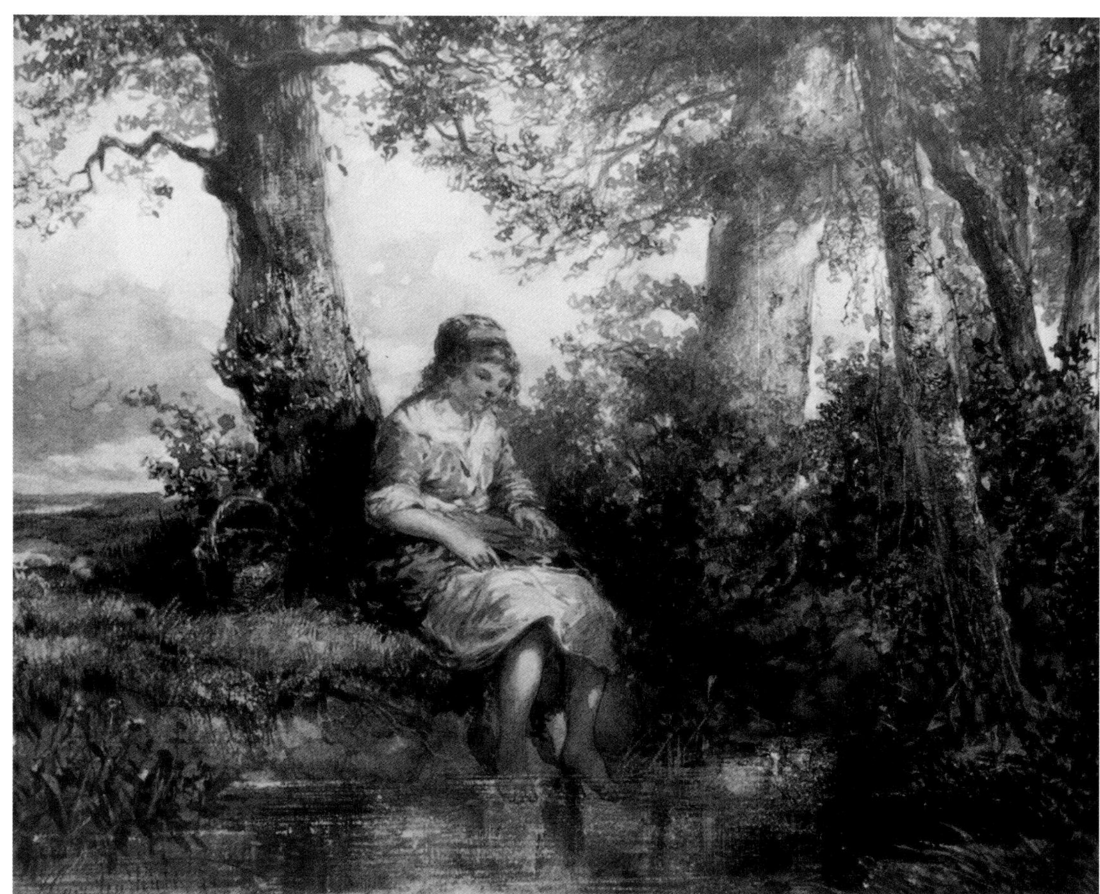

Hermanus Koekkoek

Middelburg 1815–1882 Haarlem

16. *Seascape*

Black ink and gray wash, 115 x 171 mm (4⅝ x 6¾ in.)
Signed lower right: *H. Koekkoek f*

A painter of landscape (especially rivers) and marine views, Hermanus Koekkoek was highly regarded during his lifetime. He belonged to the second of a five generation family of artists and was the son and pupil of Johannes Hermanus Koekkoek (1778–1851). In reputation he probably is second only to his older brother, Barend Cornelis (1803–1862). He lived and worked in Durgerdam, Amsterdam, Niewen-Amstel, and Haarlem where he died. He became a member of the Amsterdam Royal Academy in 1840 and the Rotterdam Genootschap in 1841.

Marine views figure prominently in Koekkoek's drawings and are the type of work for which he earned his reputation. Comparable pieces with calm seas—as opposed to choppy, stormy, or rough—can be found in the Historisch Museum (cat. 1863, no. 476) and Rijksprentenkabinet at Amsterdam and on the art market at The Hague in 1970 (photograph RKD).

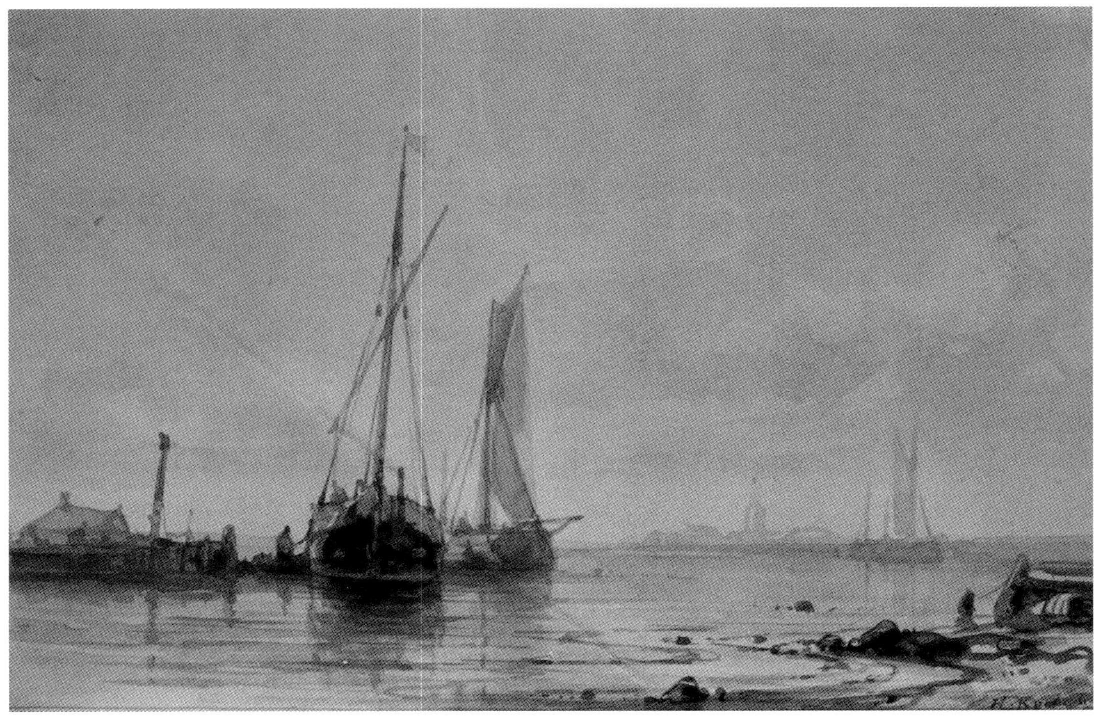

The Hague 1633–1688 The Hague

17. *Two Peacocks on the Terrace*

Pen and brown ink and wash, 222 x 355 mm (8⅝ x 14 in.)

Johan Leemans was a still-life painter: birds, birdcages, and various tools for catching birds are prevalent in his work. Crisp lines, precisely cast shadows, and minute detail give a trompe l'oeil effect to this work, which is attributed to Leemans.

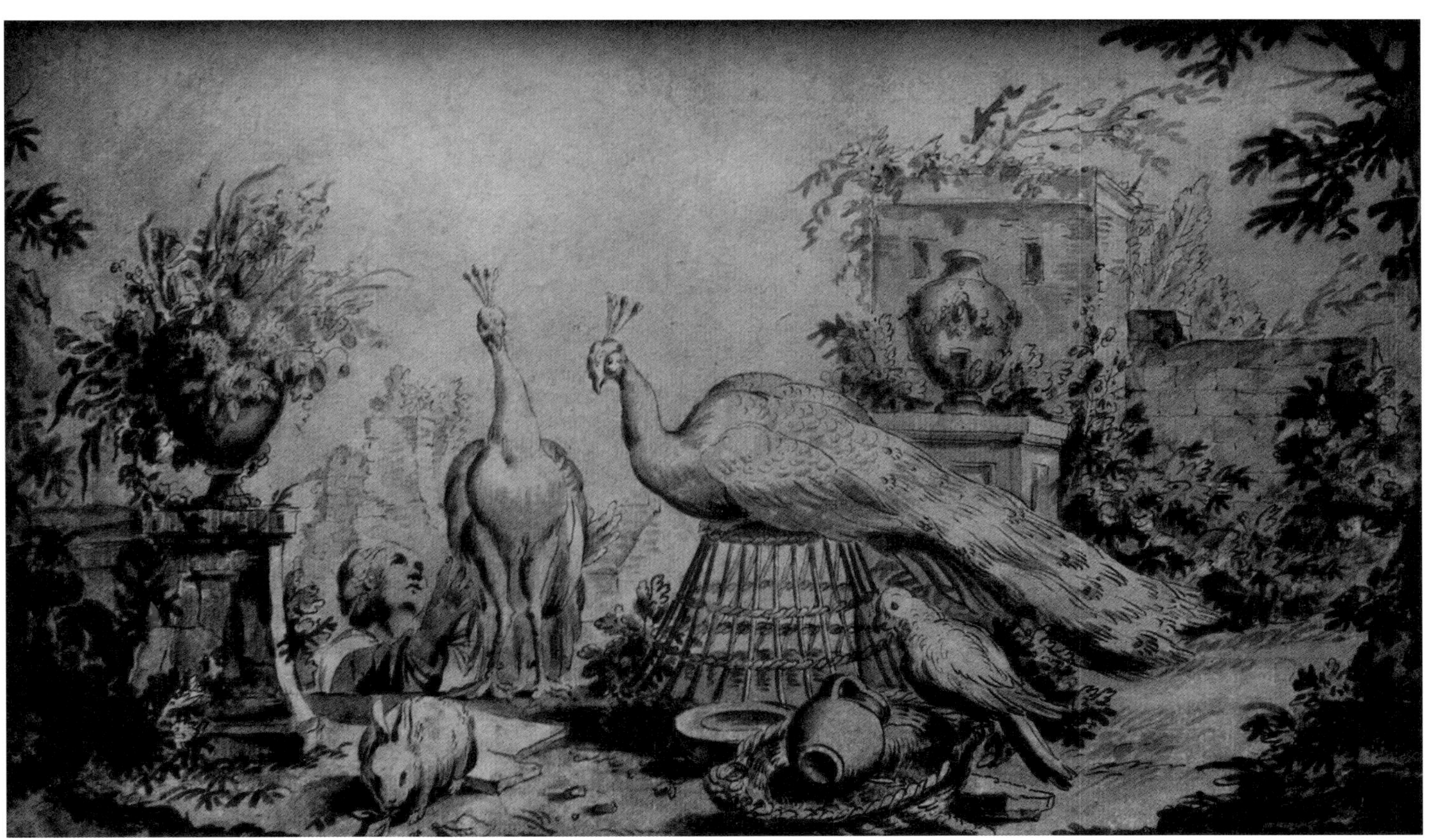

Leiden 1607–1674 Amsterdam

18. *Wagon on the Way,* about 1650s or 1660s

Pen and brown ink and wash, 187 x 216 mm (7⅜ x 8½ in.)
Signed lower right: *Jan Lievens f*

Jan Lievens studied with Pieter Lastman (1583–1633) at Amsterdam in about 1617–19. After he returned to Leiden, he shared a studio with his friend Rembrandt van Rijn (1606–1669) during the latter half of the 1620s. At this time Lievens concentrated on large-scale figures close to the picture plane while Rembrandt preferred smaller figures set within an atmospheric space. In 1632 he traveled to England and painted portraits of the royal family. Three years later he moved to Antwerp where he was influenced by Anthony van Dyck (1599–1641). In 1644 he moved to Amsterdam, remaining until his death. Lievens's drawings consist primarily of two types: portraits and landscapes drawn from nature. They are found in major collections of Dutch drawings throughout Europe.

More than one hundred fifty landscape drawings by Lievens are known, and they are executed primarily or exclusively with the broad-nibbed reed pen.[1] For the most part they were intended as finished works made for sale. Werner Sumowski has emphasized that since not a single dated example is known, chronology is a problem.[2] However, it can be determined that none date from the Leiden period and most belong to the 1650s and 1660s, which is when the Kharkiv drawing should be placed.

The rapid yet firm drawing in this work demonstrates Lievens's skill in using the reed pen. The variety of lines from short and broken to long and fluid creates a sense of movement and adds vitality to the figures and landscape. Unlike many of Lievens's landscape drawings, this work focuses more attention on the figures, animals, and cart than on dense foliage and forests.

Notes
1. Schneider and Ekkart, p. 73.
2. Sumowski, pp. 370–73.

Jan Luyken

Amsterdam 1649–1712 Amsterdam

19. *Women Spinning*

Pen and brown ink and gray wash, 86 x 75 mm (3⅜ x 2⅞ in.)

Painter, poet, and draftsman, Jan Luyken was one of the more prolific artists of the latter seventeenth century: with his son and close collaborator, Caspar Luyken (1672–1708), he left more than four thousand drawings and prints.[1] Many of his drawings were made to illustrate his own literary works including moralizing poetry, mottoes, and biblical texts.

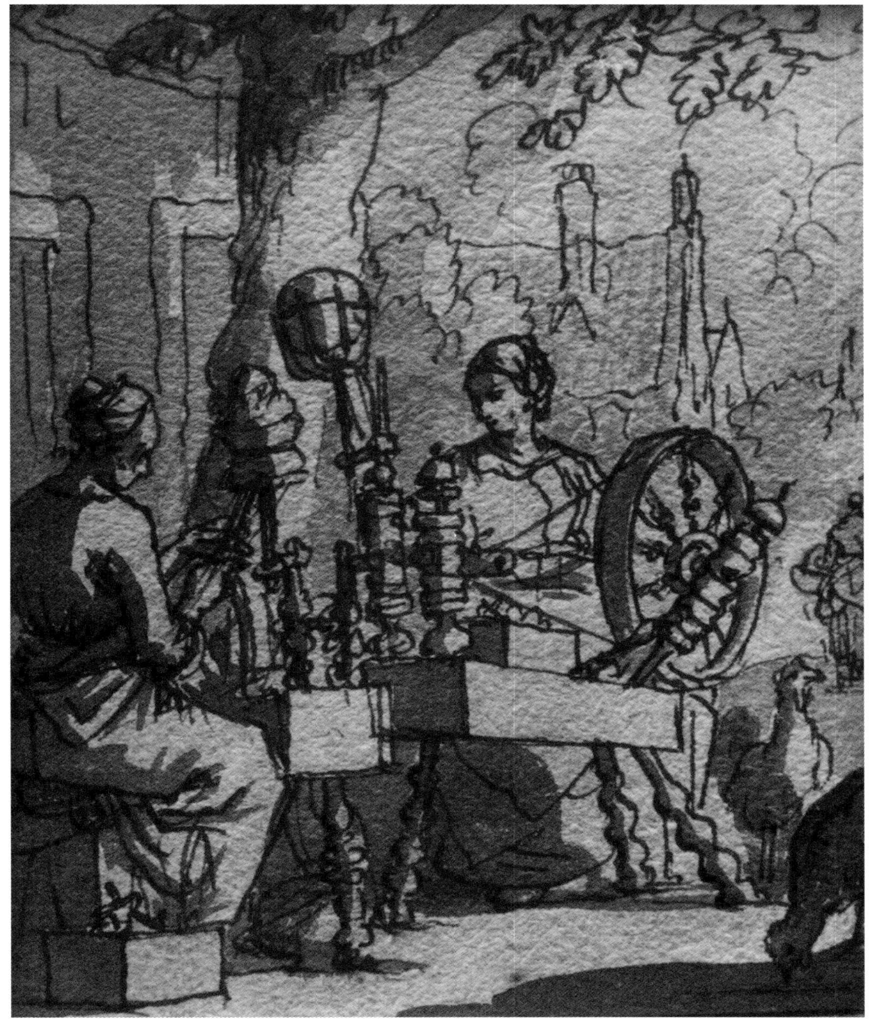

Many depict some aspect of human activity set within a landscape setting. Critical assessment is difficult because of the similarity in style of father and son and the large number of imitations produced during their lifetimes. Not all the drawings can be connected with known prints. The largest collection of Luyken's drawings is in the Historisch Museum at Amsterdam.

During the seventeenth century the motif of a woman spinning, found in both paintings and prints, functioned as a representation of domestic virtue. Spinning was one of the tasks that seventeenth-century writers considered the most important for women to practice, citing references from the Bible and texts from classical antiquity to substantiate their view. Because the actual practice of spinning was probably in decline during the seventeenth century, images of spinners represented an ideal vision of the virtuous housewife.[2] Given Luyken's proclivity for illustrating moral ideas, this drawing may be connected with one of his many text-oriented projects.

Notes
1. Van Eeghen and Van der Kellen.
2. Franits, pp. 29–31, 71–76.

Dirk Maes

Haarlem 1659–1717 Haarlem

20. *Hunters*

Watercolor, 170 x 252 mm (6¾ x 9⅞ in.)
Signed lower middle: *D. Maas*

Dirk Maes preferred subjects that included cavalry skirmishes, hunting parties, and horse fairs. He was a pupil of Hendrik Mommers (1623–1693) and Nicolaes Berchem (1620–1683). Maes was also a close friend of Jan van Hutchenberg (1647–1733), whose style he adopted. In 1678 he entered the Guild of Saint Luke at Haarlem and later moved to The Hague, entering the guild there in 1697. He accompanied William III, prince of Orange Nassau, to England and on his Irish campaign but was back in the Netherlands by 1693, continuing to work for William III. A substantial collection of thirty-three of his drawings of cavalry battles and military maneuvers can be found at the Staatliche Graphische Sammlung in Munich.[1]

Nearly all Maes's paintings and drawings contain horses, including this work. As in many of his other pieces, the setting is Italianate complete with fountains, but the costumes are northern. Also typical is the green color scheme. The identical grouping of figures, but without the trees and with an extension on the right, appears in a drawing in the Albertina, Vienna, signed *D. Maes* (no. 10380).

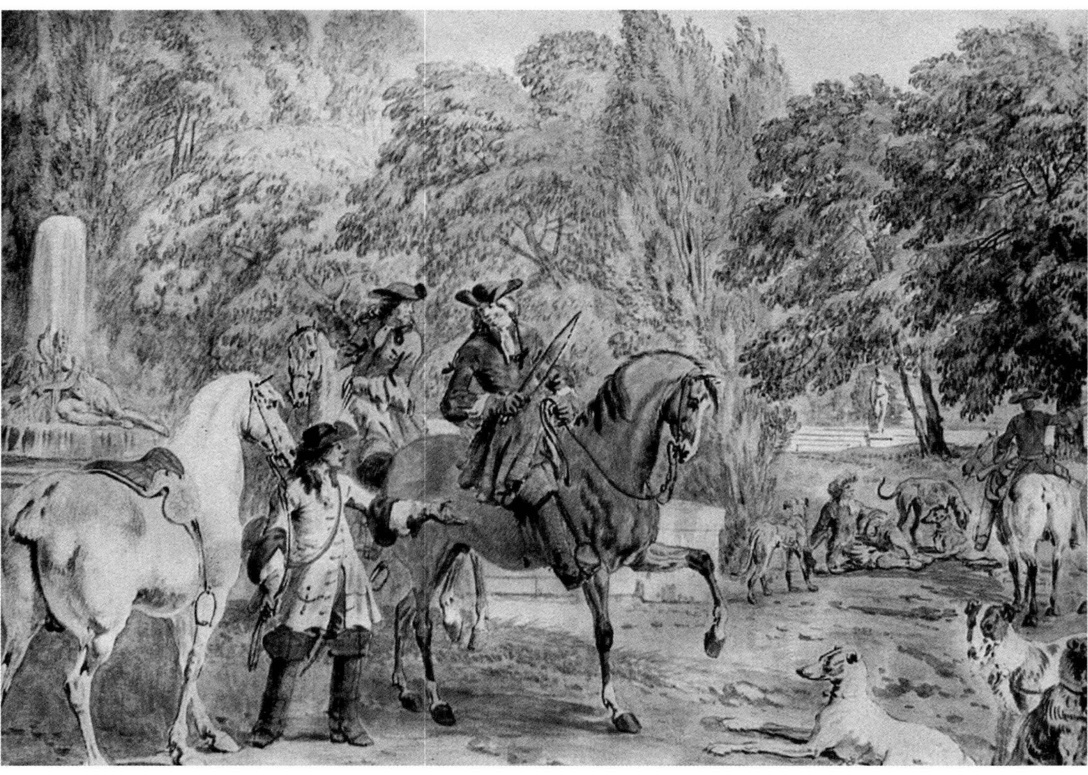

Plate VII

Note
1. Wegner, pp. 102–4, nos. 708–41.

Anton [Antonij] Mauve

Zaandam 1838–1888 Arnhem

21. *Cows*, 1858

Watercolor over traces of graphite, 239 x 333 mm (9¼ x 13 in.)
Signed and dated lower right: *A. Mauve f 58*

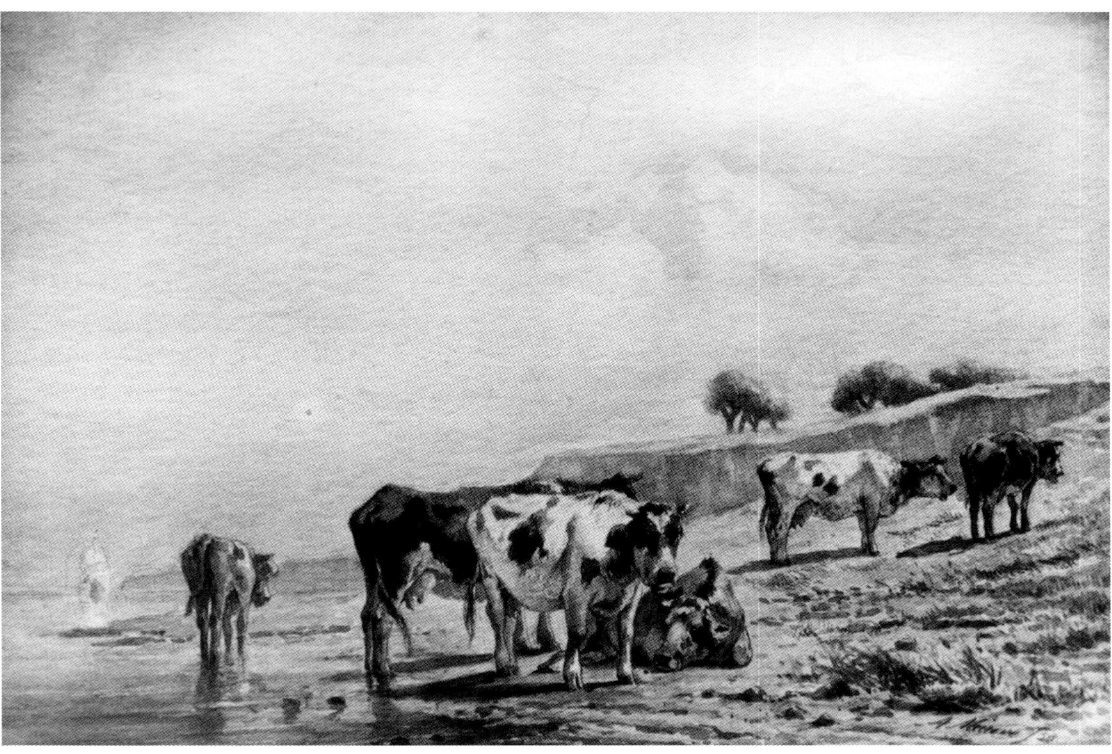

Anton Mauve was an artist of everyday subjects. A superb watercolorist, he had a sincere respect for this medium and for drawing in general and helped to establish the Dutch Drawing Society in 1876. He was a pupil at Haarlem of the animal painter Pieter Frederik van Os (1808–1892), who gave him a good grounding in technique, and Wouterus Verschuur (1812–1874), who painted horses and stables. His clear understanding of animal anatomy served him well throughout his life. Mauve lived and worked in Haarlem (1856–68), Amsterdam (1870), The Hague (1872–85), and Laren (1886–88). He gave his works a melancholic air by limiting his palette, probably through the influence of the French artists Jean-François Millet (1814–1875) and Charles-François Daubigny (1817–1875). A relative of Vincent van Gogh (1853–1890), Mauve was his first teacher. Throughout his life Van Gogh remained indebted to Mauve for his guidance with regard to watercolor techniques and life drawing. Major collections of Mauve's drawings and watercolors can be found in the Rijksmuseum and Rijksprentenkabinet at Amsterdam, the Rijksmuseum Kröller Müller at Otterlo, and the Gemeentemuseum at The Hague.

This work may have been produced while Mauve was a pupil of Verschuur in 1858 or during the summer months when he stayed with Paul Gabriël (1828–1903) in Oosterbeek, where he lived on and off until 1874.[1] Mauve excelled in watercolor, and the present example shows his delicate and evocative style. He includes no figures and instead uses the cows to define space and content. Especially outstanding are the way he plays line against light and shade in the definition of the cows and the manner in which the spotted white cow in the foreground is set against the darker cow. Brown-and-white cows are typical of the Oosterbeek region. Landscape elements are kept to a minimum but serve to enhance the mood, which pays tribute to some of the great seventeenth-century Dutch painters of animals, in particular Paulus Potter (1625–1654).

Note
1. Sillevis, pp. 6–7.

Peter Molijn

London 1595–1661 Haarlem

22. *Landscape with Figures,* 1654

Black chalk and gray wash, 150 x 195 mm (5⅝ x 7⅝ in.)
Signed and dated upper right: *P Molyn 1654* (*P* and *M* in monogram)

Peter Molijn was a painter, draftsman, and etcher. He was a member of the Guild of Saint Luke in Haarlem. Together with Esaias van de Velde (about 1590–1630) and Jan van Goyen (1596–1656), he was a pioneer in the development and depiction of the Dutch landscape in art during the seventeenth century. He mainly painted images of his neighborhood in Haarlem and imaginary mountain landscapes. Molijn was also the instructor of Gerard ter Borch (1617–1681) and probably Allaert van Everdingen (cats. 8, 9).

With the exception of a few pieces, nearly all Molijn's drawings were executed in black chalk with gray or brown wash and created with the intention of selling them to collectors. Most of these were produced during the 1650s, with large numbers produced in 1654, 1655, and 1659. Molijn preferred sheets of about 150 by 190 millimeters in 1654 and 1655, and sheets measuring 190 by 300 millimeters in the latter 1650s, suggesting that many of the landscapes were issued in series.[1] His style is close to that of Van Goyen (compare cat. 11). Molijn's drawings are found in major collections of Dutch art throughout Europe.

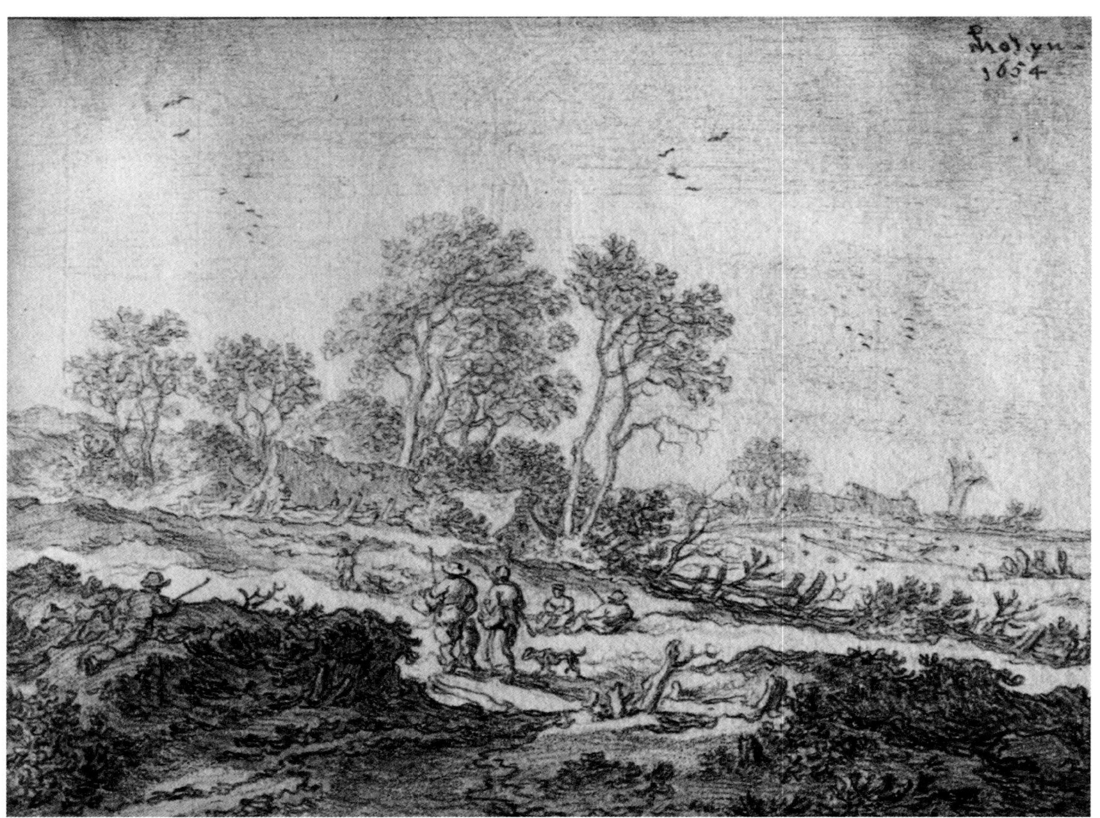

Hans-Ulrich Beck has shown that the exhibited work is authentic but one of Molijn's duplicate drawings, of which there are about thirty known at present—an unusual situation among Dutch drawings of the seventeenth century.[2] The drawing is typical of Molijn's work in the mid-1650s with its nervous black chalk line, undulating terrain, windswept trees, and integration of everyday life into the landscape. Molijn frequently shows figures from behind, and in this drawing the placement of the two hunters in the middle ground bathed in sunlight effectively serves to lead the viewer into the landscape and contrasts with the darker areas of land in the foreground. Drawings such as this one were executed in the studio probably based on sketches from nature made earlier.

Notes

1. Robinson, in Robinson and Schatborn, p. 86.

2. Beck IV, no. 764, A7; and letter to the author, 11 Jan. 1996. Beck's study of the duplicate drawings by Molijn will appear in a forthcoming article in *Master Drawings*.

Amsterdam 1667–1744 Amsterdam

23. *Forest Landscape,* 1738

Black chalk and watercolor, 230 x 343 mm (9⅛ x 13⅜ in.)
Signed and dated lower left: *Moucheron fecit. 1738*

Isaac de Moucheron was primarily a painter and draftsman of landscape. He was the son and pupil of Frederick de Moucheron (1633–1686) and grandson of Isaac Jouderville (about 1612–before 1648), who was a pupil of Rembrandt (1606–1669). He studied in Italy about 1695–97 and belonged to the group of northern artists in Rome known as the Schildersbent (band of painters). From them he received the "Bent" name Ordonnantie

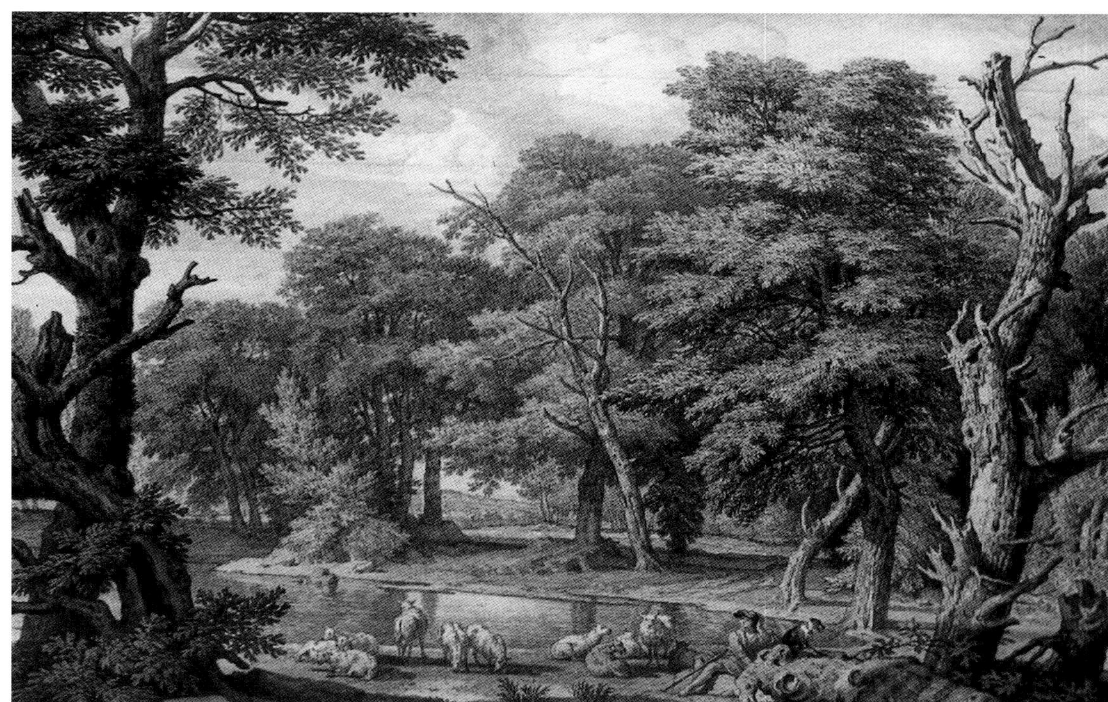

Plate VIII

(arranger) because of his skillful compositions.[1] He specialized in vedute (scene painting), and his landscapes exhibit an emphasis on detail and truthfulness of depiction. Much of his work reveals the influence of the French classicist masters, especially Gaspard Dughet, called Poussin (1615–1675). He is known as well for his wall decorations made for wealthy patricians' houses, where he introduced new themes based on parks with prominent architectural features. He was likewise an important draftsman and produced preparatory studies and finished drawings in watercolor. His skill as a colorist was so highly regarded that many collectors asked him to add color to their seventeenth-century drawings.

Moucheron's style characterizes the change in spirit in Holland from the seventeenth to the eighteenth centuries with increased emphasis on refinement. His handling of the trees in this work, with their full foliage and elegant trunks, is typical of his landscape drawings. In addition Moucheron liked to play dead trees against those that are in full leaf creating decorative patterns that unify the drawing.

The motif of the shepherd and the handling of the trees are close to those in a drawing formerly in the collection of Emile E. Wolf, New York.[2] Most of Moucheron's known drawings were executed in pen and ink and watercolor, with important examples in the Kunsthalle at Hamburg, the Albertina at Vienna, and the Rijksmuseum at Amsterdam.

Notes
1. Blankert, pp. 245–46.
2. Exhibited in Dutch Drawings of the Seventeenth Century, Ithaca, 1979, no. 60; Sale, Amsterdam (Sotheby's), 10 May 1994, no. 72.

Georgius Jacobus Johannes van Os

The Hague 1782–1861 Paris

24. *Flower Bouquet*

Watercolor, 345 x 260 mm (13½ x 10¼ in.)
Signed lower left: *G.J.J. van Os F.*

Georgius Jacobus Johannes van Os painted still lifes, especially flowers and fruit, and worked primarily in watercolor. A pupil of his father, Jan van Os (1744–1808), he lived and worked in Amsterdam between 1810 and 1812. In 1812 he moved to Paris but lived sporadically in the Netherlands until 1826 when he was back in Paris where he painted a great deal for the porcelain factory at Sèvres. He continued to spend time in the Netherlands in 1834, 1840, and 1849 as well as during the summers when he worked in Haarlem. His still lifes and pictures of flowers were much sought after by collectors. Other examples are in the Historisch Museum and Stedelijk Museum at Amsterdam and the Teylers Stichting at Haarlem.

This watercolor is characteristic of the flower pieces by Van Os and reveals his mastery of composition and application of color in the watercolor medium. His attention to detail is especially noteworthy in the drops of water that cling to the leaves and flower petals and linger on the stone ledge.

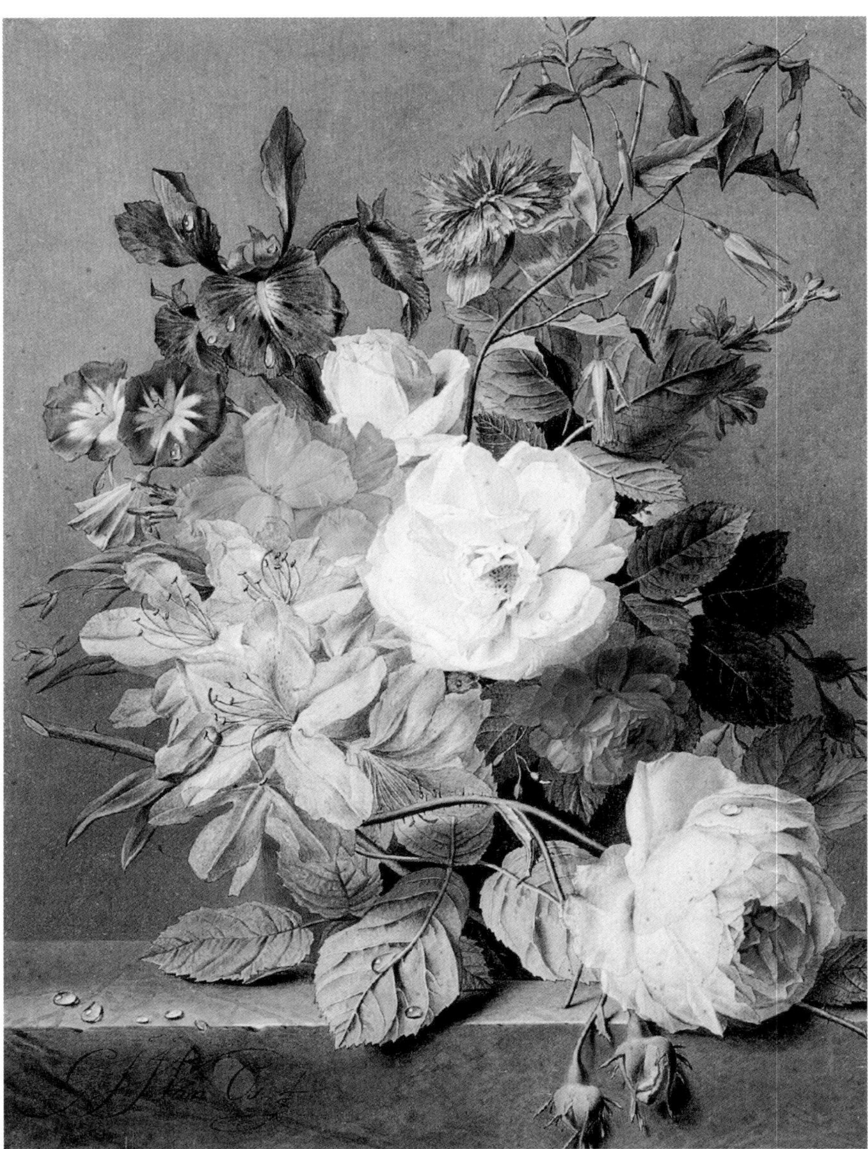

Cover

Jan van Ravenswaay [Ravenzwaay]

Hilversum 1789–1869 Hilversum

25. *Farm*, 1826

Brown wash and tip of the brush, 303 x 408 mm (11⅞ x 16 in.)
Signed and dated lower right: *JVRavenswaay fec 1826*

Jan van Ravenswaay was a landscape and animal painter. He was a pupil of Jordanus Hoorn (1753–1833) at Amersfoort and Pieter Gerardus van Os (1776–1839)—the brother of Georgius J. J. van Os (cat. 24) and well known for his landscapes and cattle pieces—at Hilversum. Van Ravenswaay visited Belgium, Switzerland, and Germany. He became a member of the Amsterdam Royal Academy in 1822 and the Arti Sacrum at Rotterdam in 1831. Van Ravenswaay took his subject matter from the

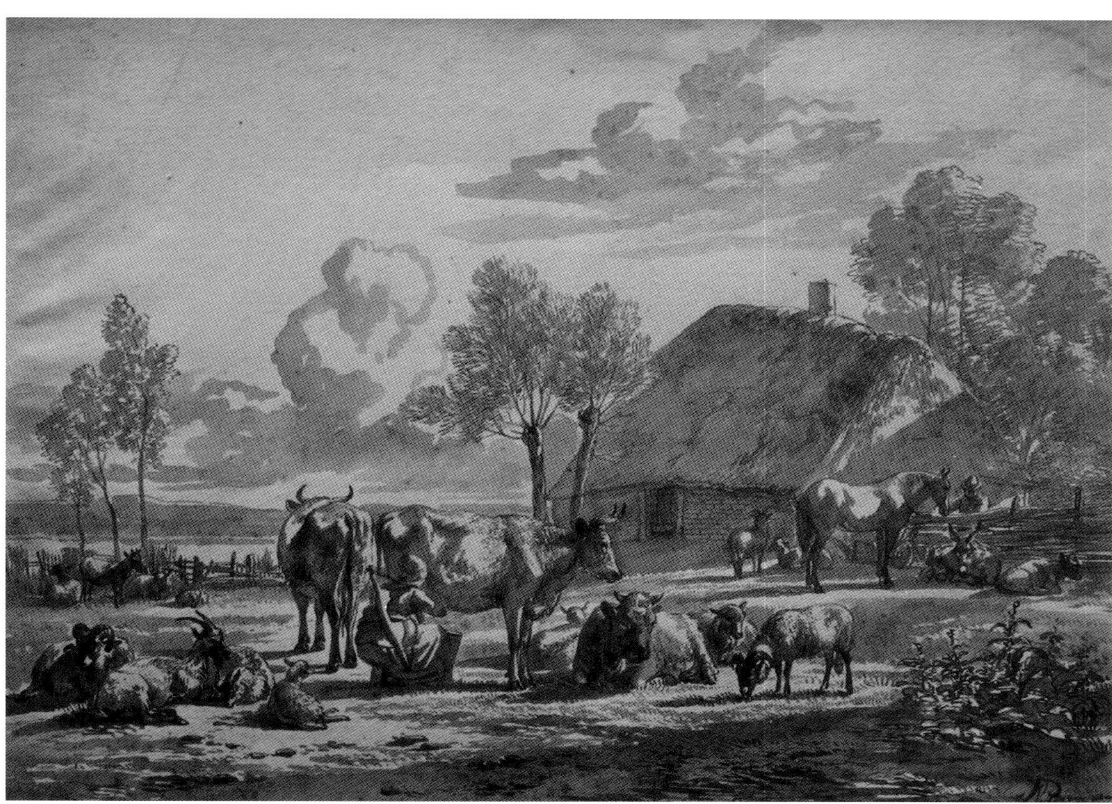

countryside around Hilversum and other sites where he visited and lived. He resided in 's-Graveland (near Hilversum) during 1810–13, stayed with his family in Drenthe between 1837 and 1847, was in Oud-Loosdrecht from 1847 to 1850, in Velp during 1852–53, and returned to Hilversum in 1855. His subjects include cattle at pasture and sheep and cows in stable scenes. In Hilversum Van Ravenswaay had a small farm of Drenthe sheep that he frequently used as models for his drawings and watercolors.[1] A significant collection of his drawings is in the Museum Boymans-van Beuningen at Rotterdam.

Ravenswaay's teacher P. G. van Os was indebted to Paulus Potter (1625–1654), the great seventeenth-century painter of animals, and that influence is evident in this work. The drawing has a luminous quality reminiscent of Potter, and the handling of light on the various animals is outstanding. Also characteristic of Potter is the manner in which the animals have been placed in the landscape to define space and to lead the viewer through the drawing. For instance, the composition moves from left to right through the linking of the reclining sheep on the left, to the two cows in the middle—one facing away from the spectator and the other parallel to the picture plane—to the next group of resting animals, and finally to the horse on the right of the drawing. Characteristic of his style are the quick, thick strokes that give life and character to the inactive sheep and standing cows.

Note
1. Sellink, in Rotterdam 1994, p. 158.

WILLEM ROELOFS

Amsterdam 1822–1897 Berchem (near Antwerp)

26. *Two Figures by a River,* 1859

Watercolor, 245 x 355 mm (9⅝ x 13⅞ in.)
Signed and dated lower left: *W.Roelofs.f1859.*
Verso: Watercolor sketch of a landscape

Willem Roelofs primarily painted landscapes featuring cows and water. He was a pupil of Hendrikus van de Sande Bakhuyzen (1795–1860) and studied at The Hague Academy during 1839–40. He lived in Utrecht and The Hague before settling in Brussels from 1847 to 1887; thereafter he lived primarily at The Hague, where he was one of the founding members of the Pulchri Studio and one of the important precursors to the Hague School painters.[1] He visited the Barbizon area of France in 1851, 1852, and 1855 and became a

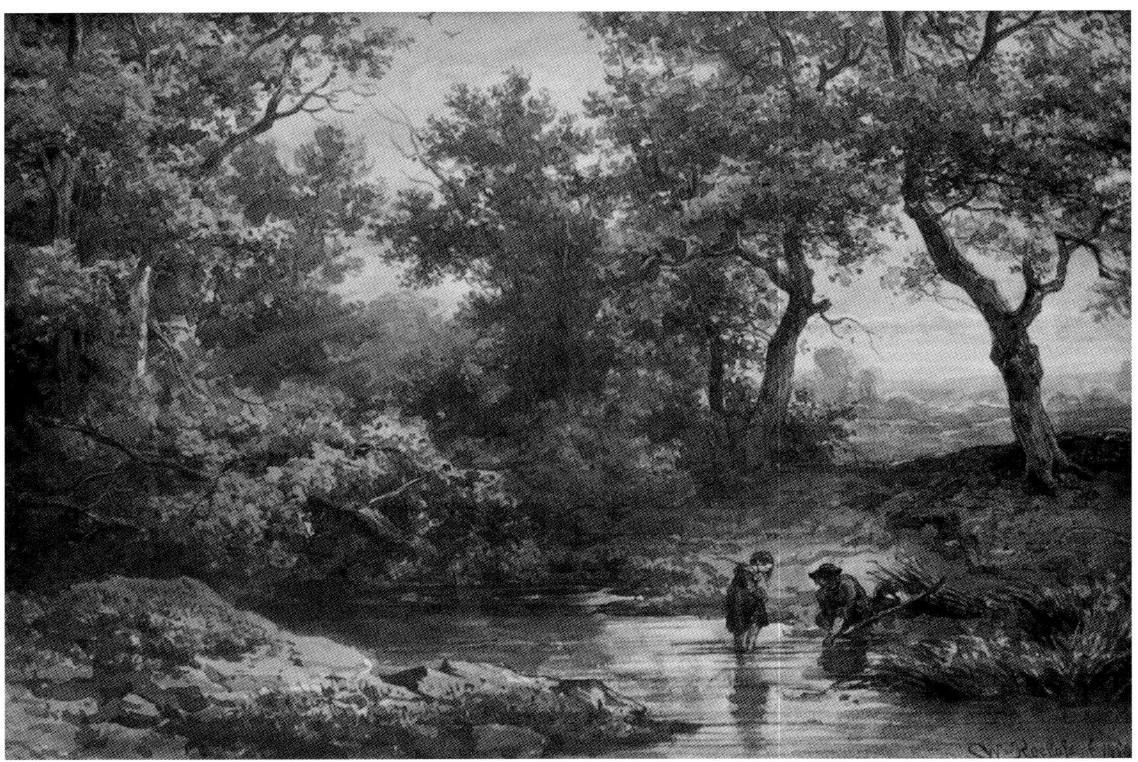

member of The Hague Academy in 1852. Primary collections of his drawings and watercolors are in the Gemeentemuseum at The Hague and the Rijksprentenkabinet at Amsterdam.

Roelofs helped to establish the Belgian Watercolor Society in Brussels and was competent in the use of the medium. His powers of draftsmanship are evident in this watercolor, which, given the date, was produced while he was living in Brussels.

During the 1850s and 1860s, Roelofs was attracted to woodland scenes, especially those around his beloved Brussels. The works produced during the early part of his sojourn in Belgium reflect the influence of Romanticism as seen in this drawing with its density, fluent brushwork, and sparkling atmosphere. After 1860 his style gradually evolved into a more realistic and analytical depiction of the world around him that was more dependent on Barbizon models.

A similar drawing with figures by a stream in a wooded landscape, signed and dated 1848, was on the art market in 1990.[2]

Notes
1. De Bodt, in Rotterdam 1995, p. 65.
2. Sale, Amsterdam (Christie's), 4 Oct. 90, no. 42, pen and ink and watercolor.

Rotterdam 1609–1685 Utrecht

27. *Peasant Woman by a Barrel*

Black chalk and brown wash, 243 x 151 mm (9½ x 5⅞ in.)
Signed in monogram lower right: *HS*

Herman Saftleven II was a painter, draftsman, and printmaker whose subjects include farmhouse interiors, imaginary riverscapes, and Italianate landscapes. He produced more than three hundred paintings, and more than twelve hundred topographical and imaginary landscape drawings have survived—for the most part finished and made for collectors. He was one of the better-known artists during his lifetime and was the subject of a panegyric published by Joost van den Vondel in 1660.[1]

Although attributed to Cornelis Saftleven (1607–1681) by the Kharkiv Art Museum, this work, based on the monogram *HS*, should be given to his brother Herman Saftleven II. In general his drawings were executed in gray or brown wash and black chalk. In style the Kharkiv drawing should be compared to two drawings by Herman in Munich showing a standing figure with hat and a young boy seen from behind[2] and two figure drawings in Leiden showing a street vendor and a young boy with rope.[3] In all five pieces the use of black chalk marks in decisive parallel strokes in combination with tonal shading is handled similarly. Likewise, the monogram on the Kharkiv drawing is comparable to that on the two drawings in Leiden.

Notes
1. Schultz 1982.
2. Wegner, p. 127, nos. 911, 912.
3. Schultz 1982, cat. nos. 1303, 1305, pls. 161, 162. For Cornelis Saftleven see Schultz 1978.

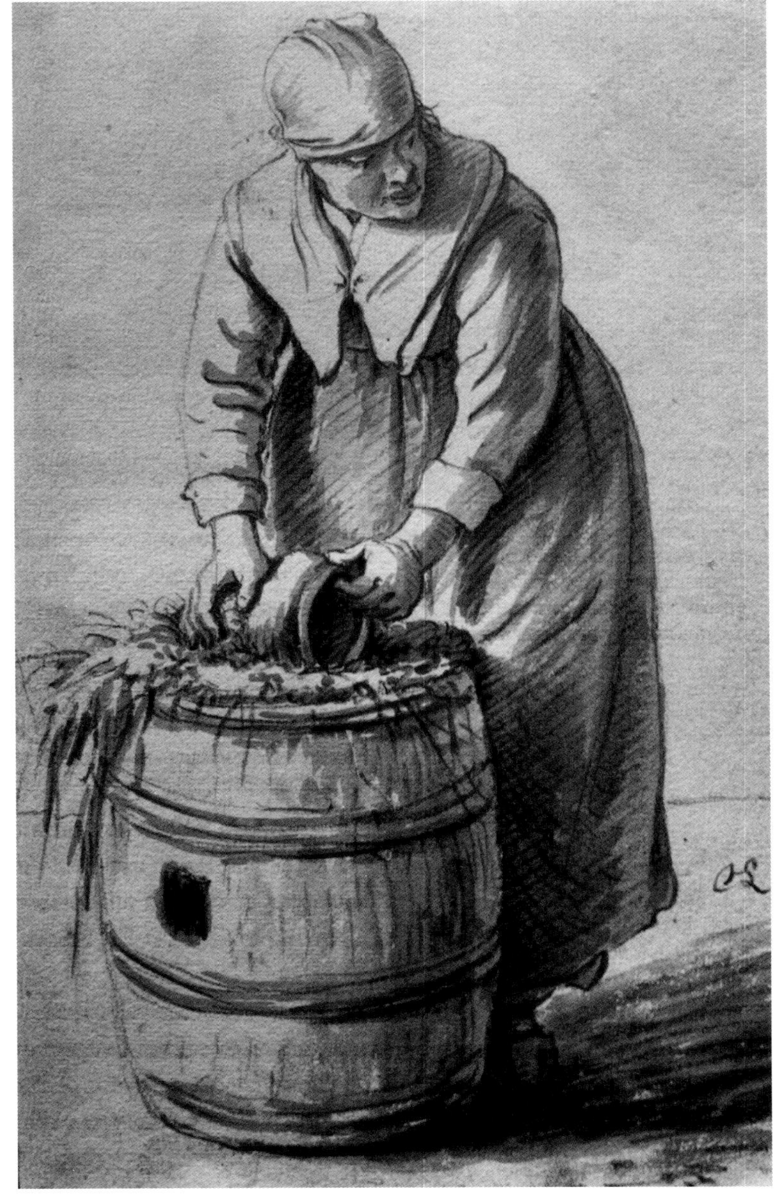

ANDREAS [ANDRIES] SCHELFHOUT

The Hague 1787–1870 The Hague

28. *Windmill and Boat in a Landscape*

Brown wash, 195 x 265 mm (7⅝ x 10⅜ in.)
Signed lower left: *A. Schelfhout*

Andreas Schelfhout was one of the better landscape artists of the Dutch Romantic period, particularly known for summer and winter scenes. He worked in his father's frame shop until his talent as a painter was recognized in 1815. His work was inspired by seventeenth-century landscape artists. He was also a talented watercolor artist, and his

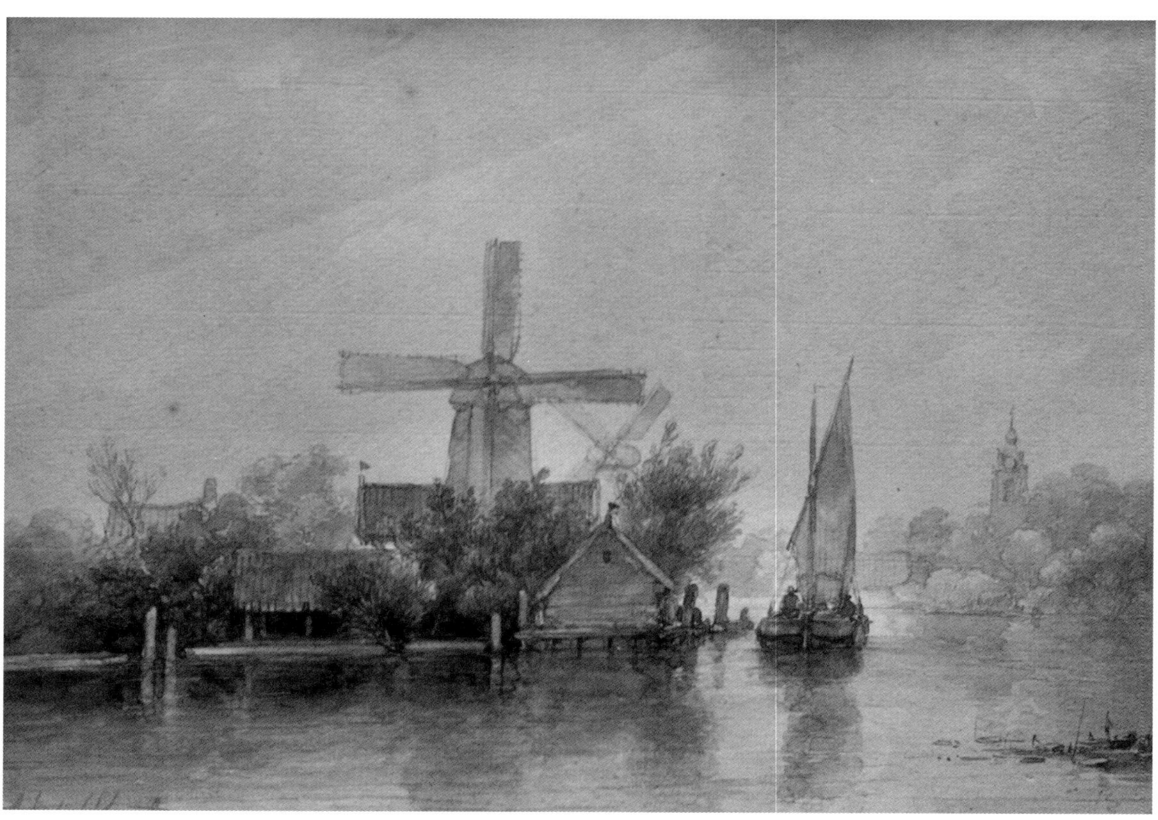

drawings are among his most graceful works. He was a member of the Pulchri Studio in The Hague. In 1830 he traveled to Paris and the north coast of France, which had the effect of changing the light and color in his watercolors.[1] According to G. Hermine Marius, his use of color puts him among the founders of the modern landscape school.[2] He gave lessons to Anton Braakman (cat. 5), Jan Frans Hoppenbrouwers (cat. 12), Johan Barthold Jongkind (1819–1891), and Jacobus Adrianus Vrolijk (cat. 34). Extensive collections of his drawings can be found in Amsterdam (Rijksprentenkabinet and Historisch Museum), Otterlo (Rijksmuseum Kröller Müller), and Rotterdam (Museum Boymans-van Beuningen).

Although this particular scene cannot be identified with specificity, the handling in the work resembles drawings of views of Leiden in the Teylers Stichting at Haarlem (cat. 266) and the Historisch Museum at Amsterdam (cat. 1863, no. 666). Schelfhout's drawings are remarkable for his handling of tonal values in the depiction of a river, buildings, and landscape. His work is characteristic of that of many early-nineteenth-century artists who attempted to create a new Dutch style based on the art of the seventeenth century. The windmill, which features prominently in this work, has been interpreted as a symbol of the Dutch nation.

Notes
1. Kapelle, in Rotterdam 1994, p. 141.
2. Marius, pp. 76–77.

GILLIS SMAK GREGOOR

Dordrecht 1770–1843 Dordrecht

29. *Landscape with Cows, Sheep, and Figures*
Watercolor, 161 x 220 mm (6¼ x 8⅝ in.)

Gillis Smak Gregoor was primarily a draftsman and painter of landscapes with cows. He lived and worked in Dordrecht. He was the nephew and pupil of Abraham van Strij (1753–1826) and also studied with Machiel Versteegh (1756–1843) and Willem van Leen (1753–1825). The Gemeentearchief at Dordrecht and the Rijksprentenkabinet at Amsterdam have substantial collections of his drawings.

Although many of Smak Gregoor's drawings include a view of his native city, Dordrecht, this work is less specific, showing animals and figures in a landscape setting.[1] Characteristic of his style, however, are the layered contrasts of light and shade, particularly on the animals, achieved through the application of colored washes. His style was indebted to the work of such seventeenth-century artists as Paulus Potter (1625–1654) and Albert Cuyp (1620–1691).

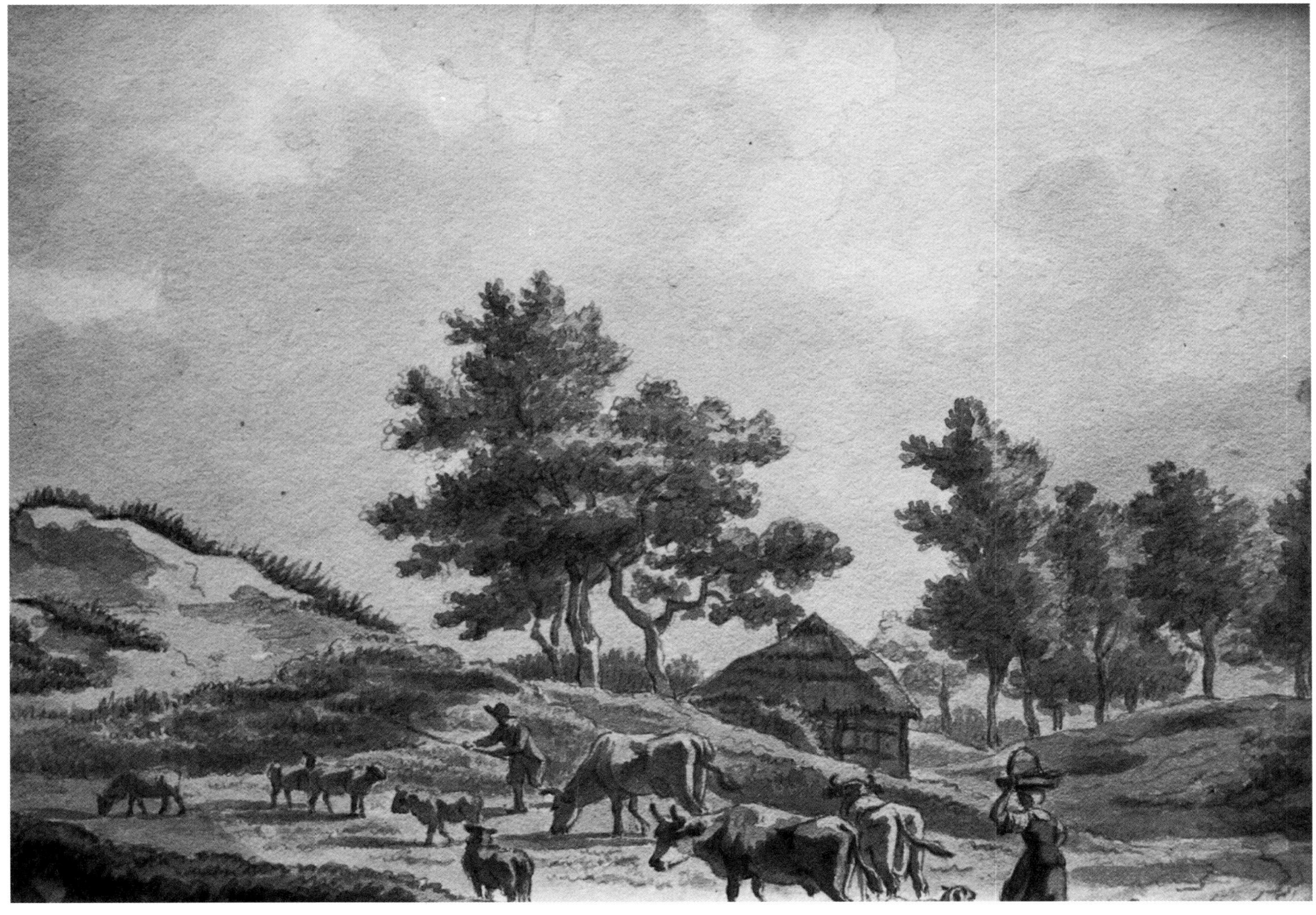

Note
1. Kranenberg, in Rotterdam 1994, p. 80.

Leiden 1633–1707 London/Greenwich

30. *Seascape*

Pen and brown ink and gray wash, 135 x 208 mm (5¼ x 8¼ in.)

Willem van de Velde the Elder was born at Leiden in 1611 and died at London in 1693. He spent his entire life making drawings of ships and small craft, which supplied the raw material for his grisailles. His drawings were mostly carried out in pen and gray wash—some tightly drawn and others more fluid—and provide a nearly complete record of ships and small craft of Holland and England during the later seventeenth century. His son, Willem van de Velde the Younger, after studying with the marine painter Simon de Vlieger (about 1600–1653), worked in close partnership with his father, first in Amsterdam and then in London where they moved in 1673. It seems that the elder Van de Velde spent time at sea making sketches of ships and maneuvers, which the younger Van de Velde used as the basis for his paintings. The latter was also a talented draftsman, and his own drawings indicate that he studied vessels of all types.[1] An important collection of the drawings of the two Van de Veldes is in the National Maritime Museum at Greenwich.

Given the closeness of father and son, it is sometimes difficult to distinguish between their work. This drawing is attributed to Willem van de Velde the Younger for its skillful pen- and brushwork that convey a vivid sense of form. Particularly effective is the manner in which the washes are used on the ships and sails to communicate the changing effects of light and shade.[2]

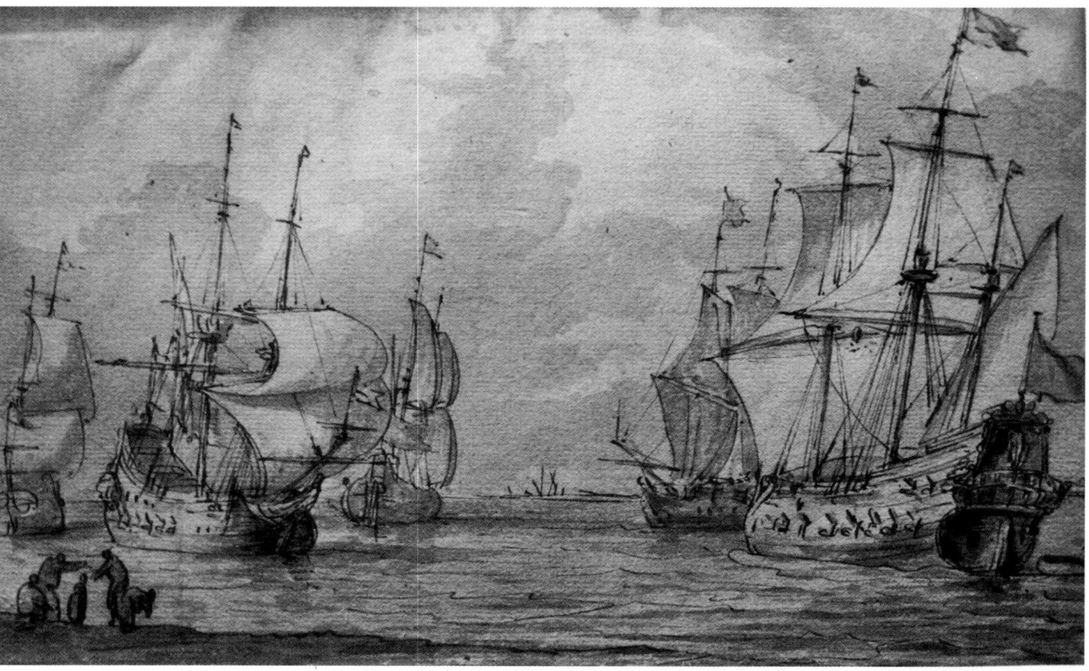

Notes
1. Cordingly, pp. 11–32.
2. For comparison see M. S. Robinson, pl. 46, no. 219, and pl. 44, no. 212.

PETRUS GERARDUS VERTIN

The Hague 1819–1893 The Hague

31. *Market in Winter,* 1850

Watercolor, 296 x 239 mm (11¾ x 9½ in.)
Signed and dated lower left: *PGVertin fc 50*

Petrus Gerardus Vertin was a painter of landscapes and town scenes, especially with light effects, who also produced etchings and lithographs. He lived and worked at The Hague. He first studied apparently with Johannes Henricus Albertus Antonius Breckenheiner (1772–1856), won a prize in 1835, and was later a pupil of Bartholomeus Johannes van Hove (1790–1880) at The Hague Academy. His drawings are also found in Otterlo (Rijksmuseum Kröller Müller), The Hague (Gemeentemuseum), and Rotterdam (Museum Boymans-van-Beuningen).

This work, which may depict a street in The Hague, is especially convincing as a winter scene in the way the snow gathers on the rooftops and window ledges. Particularly effective are the curving lines of the drooping laundry hanging from the windows contrasting with the architectural angles of the buildings.

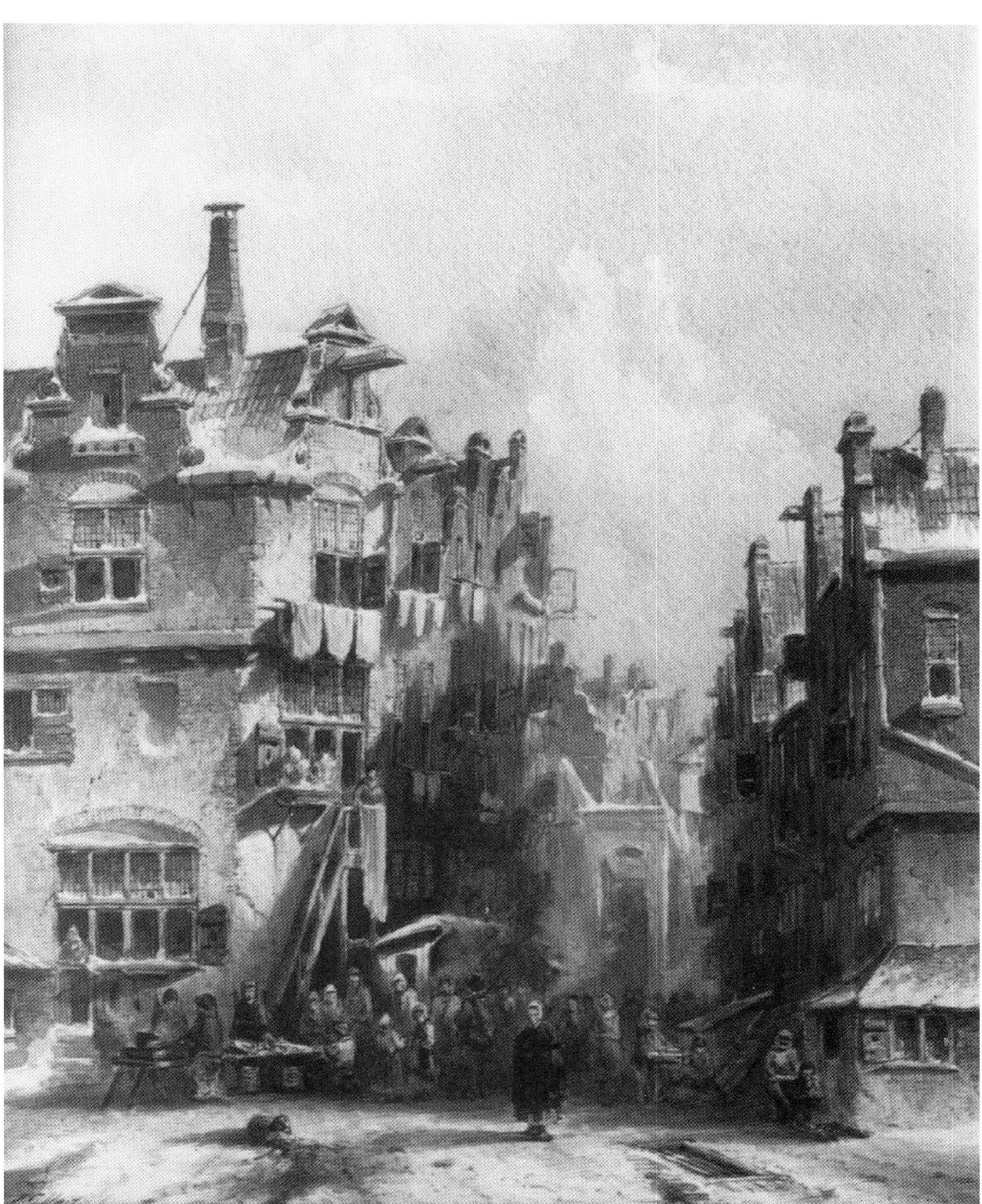

Elchanon [Leonardus] Verveer

The Hague 1826–1900 The Hague

32. *Two Children Carrying Twigs in a Landscape,* 1850

Watercolor, 198 x 228 mm (7¾ x 9 in.)
Signed and dated lower left: *Elchanon Verveer ft 50*

Elchanon Verveer was a painter of The Hague School, who lived and worked nearly all his life in that city. He was a pupil of his brother Samuel Verveer (cat. 33), Herman Frederik Carel ten Kate (cat. 14), and Louis Huard (died 1842) in Brussels. He studied at The Hague Houtgraveerschool in 1841 and at The Hague Academy during 1841–44 and 1846–48. Like Jozef Israëls (cat. 13), he took his subjects from the seacoast and the lives of fisherfolk. He was a member of the Pulchri Studio in The Hague. Other examples of his work can be found in Amsterdam (Rijksprentenkabinet), The Hague (Gemeentemuseum), Otterlo (Rijksmuseum Kröller Müller), and Haarlem (Teylers Stichting).

Verveer's watercolor landscape, executed soon after he became a member of the Pulchri Studio, serves as the perfect foil for the two girls who leave the forest warmed by the sun on their backs. The elder carries a load of twigs and walks purposefully with downcast face. Her smaller companion holds a couple of branches under one arm and gazes to the left. Verveer's deft brushwork is noteworthy for its looseness of touch and softly cast shadows, which enhance the Romantic mood of the piece.

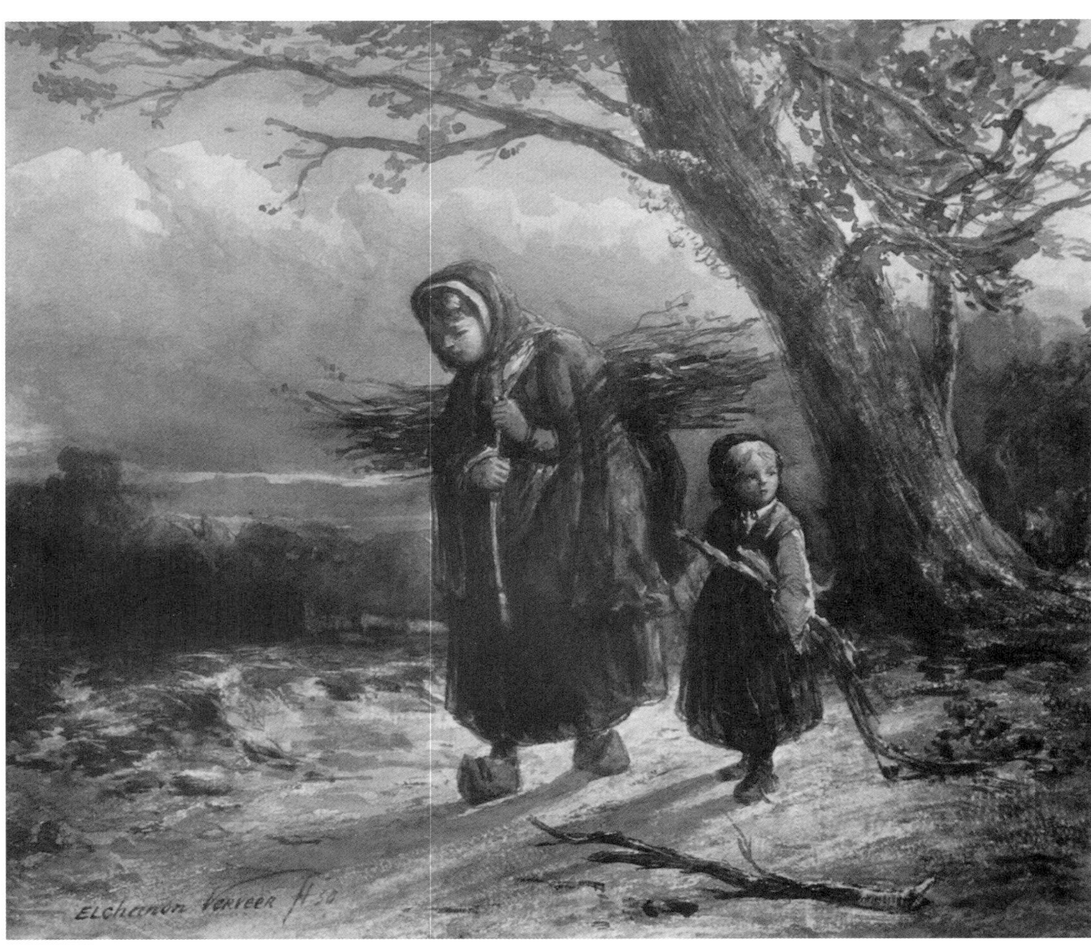

Samuel [Salomon Leonardus] Verveer

The Hague 1813–1876 The Hague

33. *Town View*

Watercolor, 92 x 134 mm (3⅝ x 5¼ in.)

Samuel Verveer was a genre and marine painter who worked in The Hague. He was a pupil of Bartholomeus Johannes van Hove (1790–1880) at The Hague Academy during 1839–43. In 1845 he became a member of The Hague Academy and also of the Pulchri Studio. He traveled to the Rhine area of Germany and France, where he spent some time in Normandy and Paris. He exhibited his work in France, Belgium, Germany, and America, where he won a medal at Philadelphia in 1876. His subject matter consisted mainly of city, village, and harbor scenes. Other collections with his work include the Rijksprentenkabinet at Amsterdam, the Teylers Stichting at Haarlem, and the Rijksmuseum Kröller Müller at Otterlo.

A watercolor drawing of a similar view was in a private collection in Scheveningen in 1965 (photograph RKD) and was once in the album of Sophie Enthoven in The Hague (1850–58).

Verveer is best remembered for his townscapes, which are often set in Jewish districts. His loose brushwork in this watercolor is in keeping with Romantic tendencies in landscape drawings at this time, and he is more interested in creating atmosphere than portraying a portrait of a particular street or building.

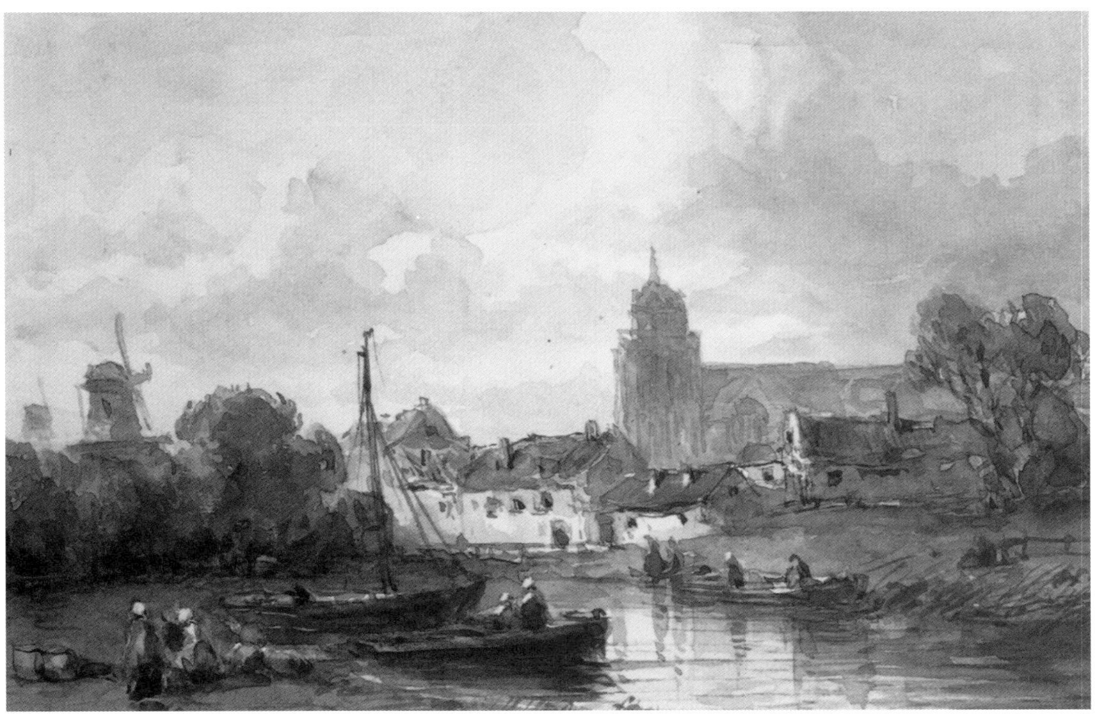

Jacobus Adrianus Vrolijk

The Hague 1834–1862 The Hague

34. *Forest*, 1861

Watercolor, 282 x 248 mm (11⅛ x 9¾)
Signed and dated lower left: *A.Vrolijk f 61*

Landscapes and town scenes were the preferred subject matter of Jacobus Adrianus Vrolijk, who was a pupil of Andreas Schelfhout (cat. 28). His brother and pupil, Jan Vrolijk (1845–1894), painted landscapes and animals. Major collections of his work can be found at The Hague in the Gemeentemuseum and Gemeentearchief.

Particularly effective in this work are the loose and dynamic brushwork and the movement of light and shade through the forest that serve to energize its mood. A similar drawing in the Boymans-van Beuningen Museum, Rotterdam, is signed with initials and dated 1850.[1]

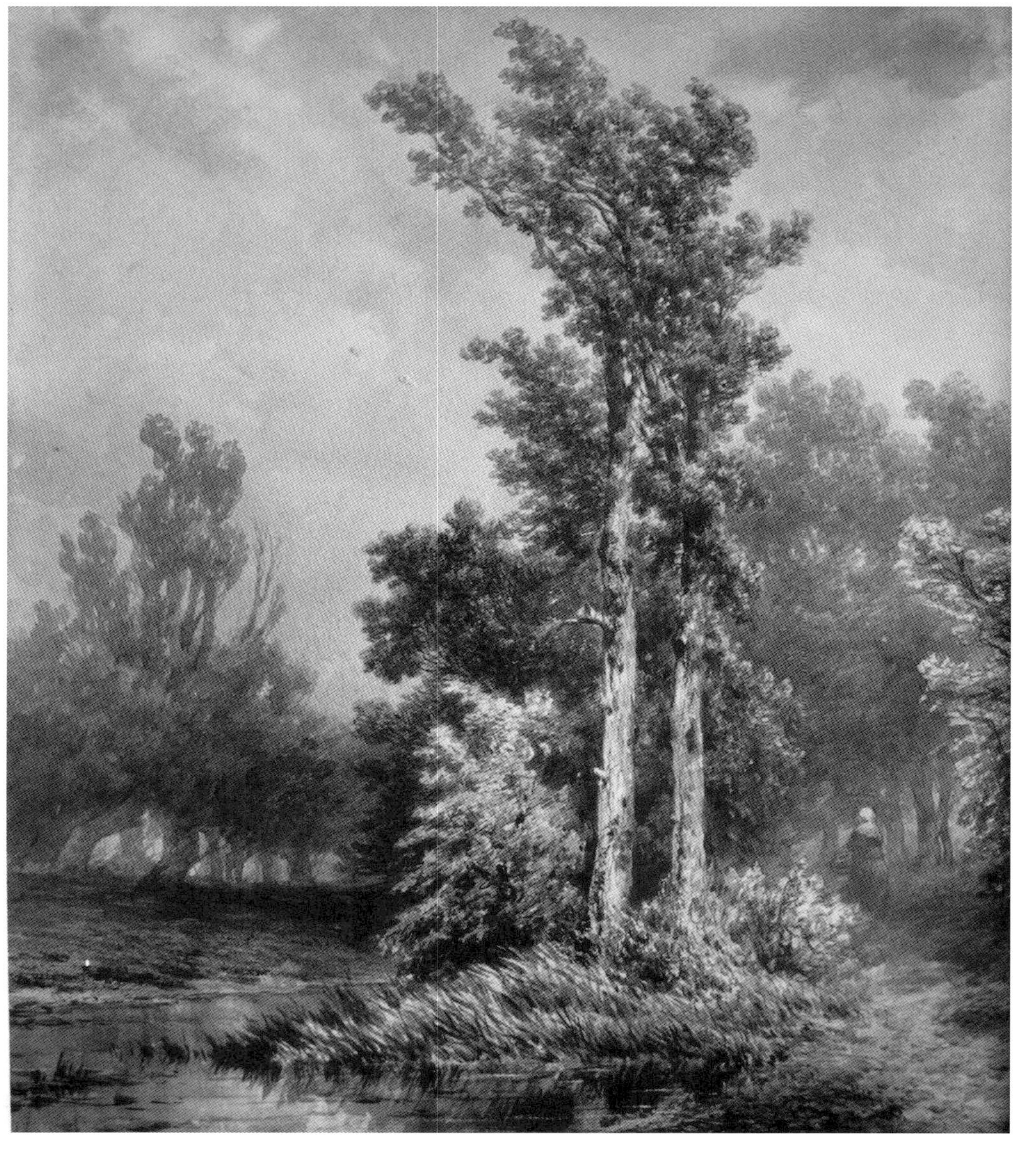

Note
1. Cat. 1994, no. 382, pen with brown and gray wash, 188 x 304 mm (7⅜ x 11⅞ in.).

Lille 1610–1690 Utrecht

35. *House in the Woods*

Black chalk and gray wash, 310 x 422 mm (12½ x 16½ in.)

Antonis Waterloo was a draftsman, engraver, and painter of landscapes, mostly forest and winter scenes. He was probably self-taught but was heavily influenced by Jacob van Ruisdael (1628/29–1682). Waterloo lived at or near Utrecht and Leeuwarden, where he was an art dealer. He traveled extensively in Europe—to Germany, Poland, Belgium, and Italy. Few of his paintings are known, and his large body of landscape and topographical drawings in black chalk and gray wash is his most important work.[1] Most of his drawings, because of their high degree of finish, appear to have been intended for sale. Other examples are in Amsterdam (Historisch Museum and Rijksmuseum), Vienna (Albertina),

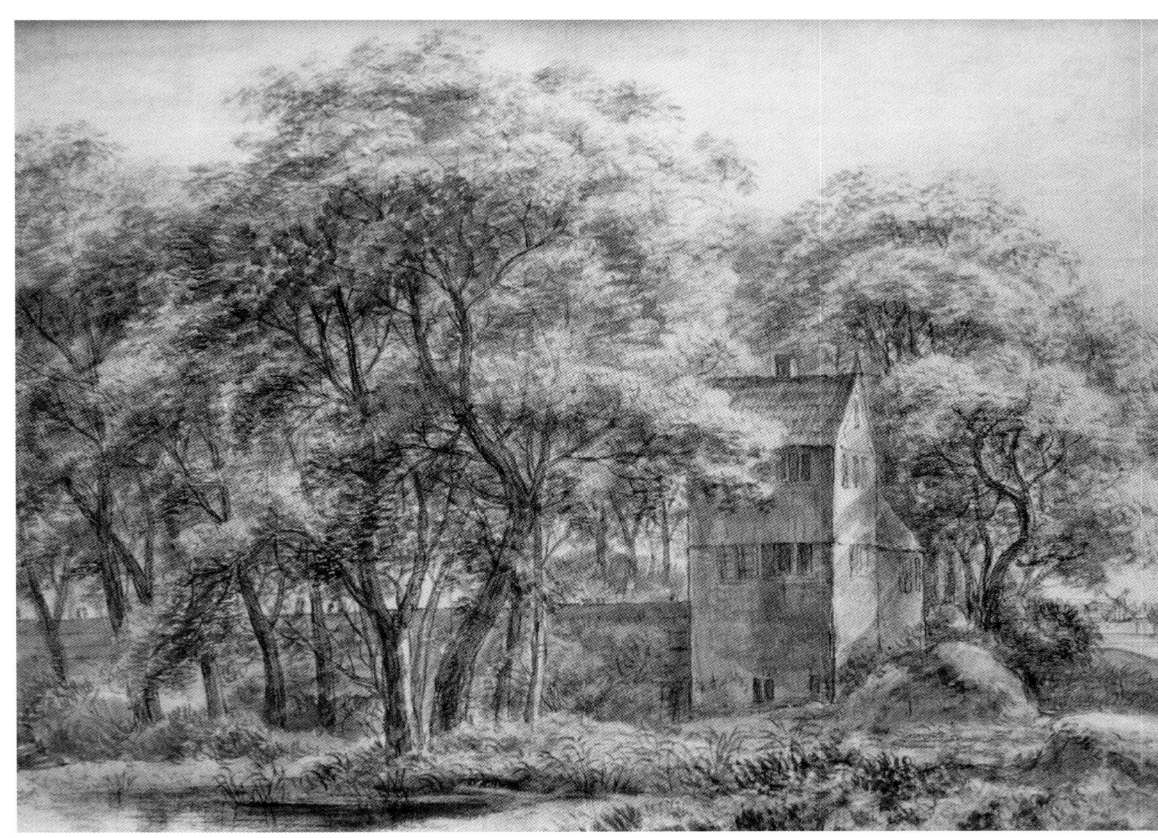

Brussels (Musées Royaux des Beaux-Arts de Belgique), Haarlem (Telyers Stichting), and Paris (Lugt Fondation Custodia, Institut Neérlandais).

Waterloo's sunlit forest scenes—including the present example—with full, vigorous trees, quiet pools, and points of architectural interest constitute a large portion of his drawn oeuvre. In this drawing his use of chalk and wash is especially effective in rendering the interaction of the tree trunks and the soft textures of the leafy trees and creating the patterns of sunlight and shade that filter through the landscape. Waterloo was successful with this type of drawing, which remained popular throughout the eighteenth and nineteenth centuries.[2]

Notes
1. Schapelhouman and Schatborn, p. 77.
2. De Wilde, p. 49.

The Hague 1822–1880 The Hague

36. *On the Square*

Watercolor, 206 x 296 mm (8 x 11⅝ in.)
Signed lower left: *Weissenbruch f*

Jan Weissenbruch was primarily a painter and etcher of townscapes—one of the best of his time. He began his studies at The Hague Academy with Samuel Verveer (cat. 33) when he was seventeen. His early work also reveals the influence of the Romantic tendencies of Wijnand Nuyen (1813–1839). He was further influenced by the topographical lithographs of the English artists Samuel Prout (1783–1852) and James Duffield Harding (1798–1863). With his cousin Jan Hendrik Weissenbruch (1824–1903), who is considered an important and esteemed artist among the Hague School, he helped to establish the Pulchri Studio. From about 1870 he suffered from agoraphobia and seldom left his studio in The Hague. One of his close friends was David Joseph Bles (cat. 3). The Historisch Museum, Amsterdam, has a large collection of his drawings; other examples are in the Gemeentemuseum at The Hague and the Rijksmuseum Kröller Müller at Otterlo.

This town scene shows attention to architectural details and overall is distinguished by active plays of light and shade. Weissenbruch's sensitivity to atmosphere and mood is enhanced by the figures dressed in historical costume.

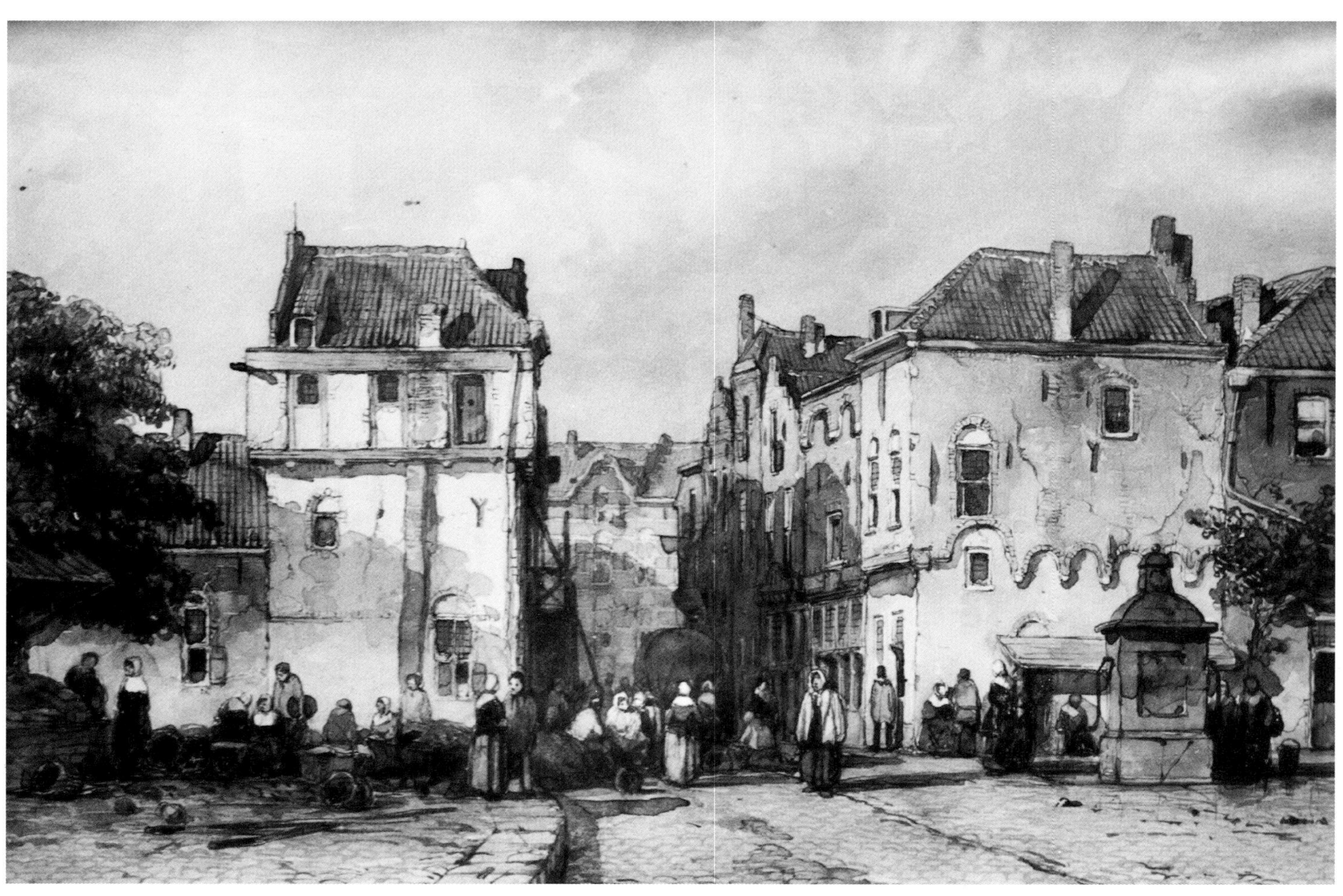

Bibliography*

Beck I–IV
Beck, Hans-Ulrich. *Jan van Goyen, 1596–1656: Ein Oeuvrezeichnis.* 4 vols. Vols. I and II, Amsterdam: Van Gendt, 1972. Vols. III and IV, Soest: Davaco, 1987.

Bernt, Walter. *The Netherlandish Painters of the Seventeenth Century.* Trans. P. S. Falla. 3 vols. New York: Phaidon, 1970.

Blankert
Blankert, Albert. *Dutch Seventeenth-Century Italianate Landscape Painters.* Soest: Davaco, 1978.

De Bodt
De Bodt, Saskia. "Pulchri Studio: Het imago van een kunstenaarsvereniging in de negentiende eeuw." *De Negentiende Eeuw, documentatieblad Werkgroep 19e eeuw* 14 (1990): 25–40.

Broos
Broos, Ben. "Improving and Finishing Old Master Drawings: An Art in Itself." *Hoogsteder-Naumann Mercury* 8 (1989): 34–55.

Brown, Christopher. *Dutch Townscape.* London: National Gallery, 1972.

Cordingly
Cordingly, David, and Westby Percival-Prescott. *The Art of the Van de Veldes: Paintings and Drawings by the Great Dutch Marine Artists and Their English Followers* (exhibition catalogue). London: National Maritime Museum, 1982.

Davies
Davies, Alice I. *Allart van Everdingen.* New York and London: Garland, 1978.

Eisler, Colin T. *Flemish and Dutch Drawings from the Fifteenth to the Eighteenth Century.* New York: Shorewood, 1963.

Van Eeghen and Van der Kellen
Van Eeghen, P., and J. van der Kellen. *Het werk van Jan en Casper Luyken.* 2 vols. Amsterdam: Frederik Muller, 1905.

Feigen
Feigen, Richard L., and Co. *Seven Highly Important Pictures Including Annibal Carracci's "The Madonna and Child with Saint Lucy and the Young Saint John the Baptist."* New York: Feigen, 1989.

Franits
Franits, Wayne. *Paragons of Virtue: Women and Domesticity in Seventeenth-Century Dutch Art.* Cambridge: Cambridge University Press, 1993.

Van Gelder
Van Gelder, Hendrick Enno. *The Changing Landscape of Holland: An Exhibition of Watercolors and Drawings of the Netherlands from 1600 to 1900* (exhibition catalogue). Vancouver: Fine Arts Gallery at the University of British Columbia, 1958.

Giltay
Giltay, Jeroen. *Kabinet van tekeningen: 16e en 17e eeuwse Hollandse en Vlaamse tekeningen uit een Amsterdamse versameling* (exhibition catalogue). Rotterdam: Museum Boymans-van Beuningen, 1976.

Van Gogh I–III
Van Gogh, Vincent. *The Complete Letters of Vincent van Gogh.* 3 vols. Boston: New York Graphic Society, 1978.

Grisebach, Lucius. *Willem Kalf, 1619–1693.* Berlin: Gebr. Mann Verlag, 1974.

De Gruyter
De Gruyter, Jos. *De Haagse School.* 2 vols. Rotterdam: Lemiscaat, 1969.

Van Hasselt, Carlos. *Rembrandt and His Century: Dutch Drawings of the Seventeenth Century from the Collection of Frits Lugt, Institut Neérlandais, Paris* (exhibition catalogue). New York: Pierpont Morgan Library, 1977.

Hollstein
Hollstein, Friedrich Wilhelm Heinrich. *Dutch and Flemish Engravings and Woodcuts, Circa 1350–1700.* 19 vols. Amsterdam: Menno Hertzberger, 1949–69.

Hurdalek
Hurdalek, Marta. *The Hague School: Collecting in Canada at the Turn of the Century* (exhibition catalogue). Toronto: Art Gallery of Toronto, 1983.

Knoef
Knoef, Jan. *Van Romantiek tot Realisme.* The Hague: A. A. M. Stols, 1947.

De Leeuw
De Leeuw, Ronald, John Sillevis, and Charles Dumas. *The Hague School: Dutch Masters of the Nineteenth Century* (exhibition catalogue). London: Royal Academy, 1983.

Logan, Ann-Marie. *The Collection of the Detroit Institute of Arts: Dutch and Flemish Drawings and Watercolors.* New York: Hudson Hills, 1988.

Marius
Marius, G. Hermine. *Dutch Painting of the Nineteenth Century.* Ed. Geraldine Norman. Suffolk: Baron, 1973 (1st Dutch ed. 1903; English trans. 1908).

Mellaart, J. H. J. *Dutch Drawings of the Seventeenth Century.* New York: Robert M. McBride, 1926.

Niemeijer
Niemeijer, J. W. *Eighteenth-Century Watercolors from the Rijksmuseum Printroom, Amsterdam* (exhibition catalogue). Alexandria, Vir.: Art Services International, 1993.

*Abbreviations for bibliography entries referenced in notes to the introductory essay or catalogue entries precede the entry and are set in italic.

Van Regteren Altena, Johan Quirijn. *Jan en Caspar Luyken* (exhibition catalogue). Amsterdam: Fodor Museum, 1933.

———. *Dutch Master Drawings of the Seventeenth Century.* New York: Harper & Brothers, 1949.

———. *Dutch Drawing: Masterpieces of Five Centuries* (exhibition catalogue). Washington, D.C.: Smithsonian Institution, 1958.

Robinson, Franklin W. *Seventeenth-Century Dutch Drawings from American Collections* (exhibition catalogue). Washington, D.C.: International Exhibitions Foundation, 1977.

Robinson and Schatborn
Robinson, William W. (catalogue), and Peter Schatborn (introduction). *Seventeenth-Century Dutch Drawings: A Selection from the Maida and George Abrams Collection* (exhibition catalogue). Lynn, Mass.: H. O. Zimman, 1991.

Robinson, M. S.
Robinson, Michael Strang. *Van de Velde Drawings: A Catalogue of Drawings in the National Maritime Museum Made by the Elder and the Younger Willem van de Velde.* Cambridge: Cambridge University Press, 1958.

Rotterdam 1994
Nederlandse tekeningen uit de negentiende eeuw 1 (exhibition catalogue). Rotterdam: Museum Boymans-van Beuningen, 1994.

Rotterdam 1995
Nederlandse tekeningen uit de negentiende eeuw 2 (exhibition catalogue). Rotterdam: Museum Boymans-van Beuningen, 1995.

Schapelhouman and Schatborn
Schapelhouman, Marijn, and Peter Schatborn. *Land and Water: Dutch Drawings from the Seventeenth Century in the Rijksmuseum Print Room.* Amsterdam: Uitgeverij Waanders, 1987.

Schatborn
Schatborn, Peter. *Dutch Figure Drawings from the Seventeenth Century* (exhibition catalogue). The Hague: Government Printing Office, 1981.

Scheen, Pieter A. *Lexicon Nederlandse beeldende kunstenaars 1750–1950.* The Hague: Kunsthandel Pieter A. Scheen, 1981.

Schneider and Ekkart
Schneider, Hans, and R. E. O. Ekkart (supplement). *Jan Lievens, sein Leben und seine Werke.* Amsterdam: B. M. Israël, 1973.

Schultz 1978
Schultz, Wolfgang. *Cornelis Saftleven, 1607–1681: Leven und Werke, mit einem kritischen Katalog der Gemälde und Zeichnungen.* Berlin: Walter de Gruyter, 1978.

Schultz 1982
———. *Herman Saftleven, 1609–1685: Leven und Werke, mit einem kritischen Katalog der Gemälde und Zeichnungen.* Berlin: Walter de Gruyter, 1982.

Sillevis
Sillevis, John. *Dutch Drawings from the Age of Van Gogh from the Collection of the Haags Gemeentemuseum* (exhibition catalogue). Cincinnati: Taft Museum, 1992.

Sluijter
Sluijter, Eric Jan. "Didactic and Disguised Meanings." In *Art in History, History in Art: Studies in Seventeenth-Century Dutch Culture.* Eds. David Freedberg and Jan de Vries, 175–207. Santa Monica: Getty Center for the History of Art and the Humanities, 1991.

Sumowski
Sumowski, Werner. "Observations on Jan Lievens." *Master Drawings* 18 (1980), 370–73.

Sutton 1984
Sutton, Peter C., Christopher Brown, Jan Kelch, Otto Naumann, William Robinson, and Cynthia von Bogendorf-Rupprath. *Masters of Seventeenth-Century Dutch Genre Painting* (exhibition catalogue). Philadelphia: Philadelphia Museum of Art, 1984.

Sutton, Peter C., Albert Blankert, Josua Bruyn, C. J. de Bruyn Kops, Alan Chong, Jeroen Giltay, Simon Schama, and Marjorie Elizabeth Wieseman. *Masters of Seventeenth-Century Dutch Landscape Painting* (exhibition catalogue). Boston: Museum of Fine Arts, 1987.

Wattenmaker
Wattenmaker, Richard J., Dedal Carasso, Boudewijn Bakker, and Bob Haak. *The Dutch Cityscape in the Seventeenth Century and Its Sources* (exhibition catalogue). Amsterdam: Historisch Museum, 1977.

Wegner
Wegner, Wolfgang. *Die Niederländischen Handzeichnungen des 15.–18. Jahrhunderts: Katalog den Staatlichen Graphische Sammlung München.* 2 vols. Berlin: Gebr. Mann Verlag, 1973.

Westerman
Westerman, Mariët. *A Worldly Art: The Dutch Republic, 1585–1718.* New York: Prentice Hall and Harry N. Abrams, 1996.

White, Christopher, and Charlotte Crawley. *The Dutch and Flemish Drawings of the Fifteenth Century to the Early Nineteenth Century in the Collection of Her Majesty the Queen at Windsor Castle.* Cambridge: Cambridge University Press, 1994.

De Wilde
De Wilde, Eliane. *Landscape in Flemish and Dutch Drawings of the Seventeenth Century from Brussels: Collections of the Musées Royaux des Beaux-Arts de Belgique, Brussels* (exhibition catalogue). Manchester: University of Manchester, Whitman Art Gallery, 1976.

Wurzbach
Wurzbach, Alfred. *Niderländischen Kunstlerlexicon . . . .* 3 vols. Vienna and Leipzig: 1906–11.